AF305217

to our parents

Produced with the generous support of
Jackie and Barry Gosin

IGOR & MARINA

SKIRA

Editor
Paola Gribaudo

Design
Marcello Francone

Editorial Coordination
Vincenza Russo

Editing
Anna Albano

Translation
Andrew Wachtel
(Ilya Kutik's essay from Russian into English)

Layout
Paola Ranzini

Iconographical Research
Paola Lamanna

Photo Credits
Marc Hauser
James Prinz
Michael Tropea

First published in Italy in 2016 by
Skira Editore S.p.A.
Palazzo Casati Stampa
via Torino 61
20123 Milano
Italy
www.skira.net

Acknowledgments
The artists would like to express their sincere gratitude
to a remarkable group of people without whom
this first monograph would not have been possible:
to Paola Gribaudo, who brilliantly curated
and edited the book, helping us in many ways long
before it even started;
to Jackie and Barry Gosin, a wonderful couple,
for their selfless generosity and moral support;
to Ilya Kutik, Associate Professor at Northwestern
University, for his beautiful essay;
to Andrew Wachtel, President of American University
of Central Asia, for translating the text into English.

Contents

Ilya Kutik

IN ******'S ALBUM

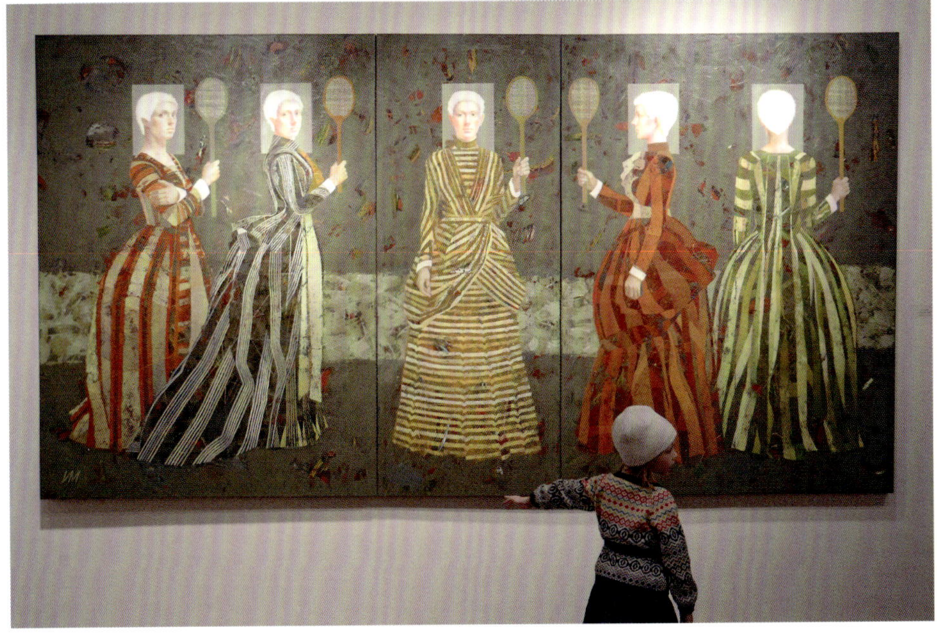

One of the opening receptions
of Igor & Marina's shows in New York

*The Exhibition, the Museum and the
Album: Horizontals and Verticals*
Toward the end of the eighteenth and
at the beginning of the nineteenth
century a new artistic genre appeared
in Russia: *the album*. The name was
given to unruled pages of quality
paper, sewn together and bound in
leather (the most popular kind was called saffian [Morocco leather], made from goat-
skin), such as can be found today at any Barnes & Noble store. But in those days al-
bums were a rarity, and in Russia they were the property of aristocratic women, who
filled them with material provided by friends and famous people: drawings, poems, and
even bits of music. Already in nineteenth-century Russia, female aristocrats were better
educated and better read than men, and were more interested in the arts, both Russian and foreign (aristocratic men, by contrast, tended to be more conversant regarding
horses, pistols, politics, duels and agriculture, than literature, visual art or opera).

One should not confuse the *album* of an aristocratic woman with her *diary*,
as these were two quite different "looking glasses" which reflected a) her social and
b) her spiritual status. In the nineteenth century the *diary* was a kind of "sentimental
journey" (after Sterne) of the mind and the soul, practically their only addressee—as
well as their confessor and interlocutor; the *album* on the other hand, was a collection
of impressions from the pens of others having to do with the album's owner and her
salon, expressed in a generically flexible form.

Thanks to the separate, that is non-overlapping, existence of the diary and the
album, a person could be reflected from two sides simultaneously: from the outside
(in the gleam of ballroom floors, the social sphere, "one's own circle") and from the
inside (alone with shiny or matte paper, as if by oneself in front of a mirror). These
two images never came together completely, but made life more 3D, as one might say
now, where the pictures (unless one wears special glasses) never fully fuse.

When, in the twentieth century, to the theoretical joy of Walter Benjamin,
the album was transformed from a private *genre* to which every major figure—from
Pushkin, Gogol and Glinka through Dostoevsky, Repin, Stravinsky, and Kornei
Chukovsky—had contributed at one time or another, to a book with an edition of
a certain size, our understanding of its uniqueness and particularity changed: after
all, when we use the word album today, what do we mean? Is it a published (that
is, already imprinted on shiny paper) collection or selection of paintings, drawings,
photographs with certain accompanying texts (as in the case of this book)? Or is it
a file on an iPad, a computer which almost everyone has? Or is it simply an object,
like a beautiful little vase and cookies at a late afternoon gathering (they aren't called
coffee table books for nothing), to give people something to do with their hands and
eyes when *small talk* doesn't flow?

In any case, the album, having ceased to be a part of private life, has become *information*. Sometimes with *hyperlinks*, creating its "vertical slice". Since art, like information about art, is not just a trunk, but also *branches*, to say nothing about roots; it is not merely *horizontals* (perspective), but also a *well* (depth). In this essay about the Russian artists Marina Sharapova (born 1960) and Igor Kozlovsky (born 1956), I will speak about "wells" and "branches". That is, about how to *read* their paintings in depth and on the surface.

When we look at paintings on the walls of an exhibition or a museum, we look at them as we do people; straight on, face-to-face, horizontally. We do not and cannot see what is beyond—behind the heads of those people and the backs of the paintings—a crowd or a street, or just a blank wall.

Looking at pictures in an album, we look down on them from above—that is almost into their depths. If we look, for example, at Kazimir Malevich's *Black Square* on a museum wall, it is possible to guess how and why we are seeing a "new icon" (as the artist himself believed), but if we look at it in an album it is easier to imagine oneself to be a bird, flying over the rectangular square of a skyscraper heliport.

Beneath the heliport's black asphalted square is an entire skyscraper, whose height is not visible, just as we don't see the long history of icon painting in the "black square" on a white piece of canvas and on a white wall. In order to understand that, we would need to know that the icon frame, stripped of its "board" painted with a celestial image, shines with the same holy blackness as does Malevich's painting, that the outline (or silhouette) of a Christ the Savior or a Madonna and Child that has been carefully cut out of its frame (but only the hands and faces) is no less sacred than the original icon. But does *everyone* who looks at *Black Square* <u>need</u> to know this? It is not necessary, but—in order to avoid silly phrases like "I could have made that myself!"—it helps.

Malevich, the Icon, and the Frame
Looking at the paintings of Igor & Marina (the nom de plume, as it were, of Igor Kozlovsky and Marina Sharapova) it is pretty unlikely that anyone would say that he or she could make them like they do. *No way!* Because what we have here is the quintessence of what has in our day been basically forgotten—the personification of art, true visual craftsmanship, artifice, and artistry—which had seemingly been lost forever in the development of the world of painting: from personal touch and uniqueness (its *madeness*) to the apotheosis of *ready-made* art at the end of the twentieth century.

At the same time, there is no way one would want to call this art "old-fashioned". But in order to truly understand how a given new thing relates to so-called "old" things—an understanding that can only come through comparison—we will have to return, again and again, to Malevich and the Russian icon.

As has already been noted, a Russian icon consists of two parts: the board and the frame. On the board an image is drawn (in color, painted), while the frame (a type of case—made of gold or silver, or even plain metal) traces an exact but empty (yawning, "black") contour to surround the face (or faces), and also the hands. The icon is placed into the frame (case) and later (ideally), the case is given an extra and separate ornamentation made of precious stones that are supposed—both literally and figuratively, which are actually the same thing in icon painting—to emphasize the value of the icon as a whole.

The frame hides under itself (inside itself) almost the entire painted part of the icon: we see only the faces (the images) plus their hands, but we do not know about the details of their clothing (actually, they are doubled on the frame, that is from the outside, but in silver, gold and so forth, and in relief), nor about the icon's background. Thus, what is inside the frame is something sacred and mysterious surrounded by the brilliant sheen—again both literally and figuratively speaking—of gold and precious stones (the same idea of mystery surrounds the orthodox altar, which is hidden behind the gates of the iconostasis which are opened to all only on the most important church holidays and to individuals only on their wedding day).

Icons were often stolen, not because of the "quality of the painting" on the board or for their spiritual qualities, but rather in order to get hold of the precious frames and the stones set in them. The frame would be torn off and would thus disappear forever, while the icon itself would become naked (indeed, the vast majority of icons exhibited today as "works of art" are displayed precisely in this way).

This is not well known in the art world and rarely written about. But of course not everyone knows that even classical Greek statues were not originally pure white; quite to the contrary, they were carefully and artfully painted. In time the paint wore off and we inherited white and empty eye sockets instead of blue and brown-eyed gods and goddesses. And let's not forget that Zeus at Olympia and Athena on the Acropolis were, for spectators in their ago of glory, not at all naked marble but rather wore heavy gold clothing (stolen when Greece was conquered), and that his contemporaries officially brought their sculptor Phideus to trial because he either took some of that gold for himself, or did not use it as had been contemplated.

Dressing up an icon in a precious frame (chasuble) came into the Byzantine Christian tradition from Greece, and the Greek pagan pantheon of (anthropomorphized) gods and their statues were "replaced" by the Christian pantheon of saints ("sons of man") and their icons (depictions). As has already been noted, in time, the frame (the icon's "clothes") and the painted board (and the image as the center and basis of the icon) began to live completely separate lives. But given that the frame of an icon is still considered an icon even without the board underneath it, it is a metaphysically sacred object even in the absence of the board; that is, even without a face and presenting only a "black" silhouette (see the illustration on the left).

However (and this is important for us), the cut out space in the frame is by no means a silhouette in the normal or even artistic use of the term. Because a silhouette is also an artistic genre: it was popular beginning in the eighteenth century (in parallel to the genre of the album) in both Europe and Russia. And even earlier, in China and Japan; let's recall the paper puppets of the "shadow theater" that exist to this very day. It is also worth noting that the bas-reliefs of classical Greece usually portrayed subjects in profile, as would all future versions of silhouette art.

But in an icon of the Greek type, the silhouette/cut outs show objects only *en face* (that is they show the contours of heads, looking directly at the viewer). This is important first of all because from a "black" profile of a person (a face or figure) one can get much more information than from the silhouette of a single head, which provides a formal prod to the imagination but no information. That is why Malevich called his *Black Square* a new icon—it is precisely a cut out space in the frame of an icon, the board with the image having been removed. In its place our imagination is free to place any one— from the most profane face to nothing at all (the emptiness of the Dao or Nietzsche's "God is Dead") to the most sacred, even if that sacred image expresses nothing but our horror in the face of the yawning mystery of all being. But let's not forget that in addition to *Black Square*, Malevich also painted his *White Square* on white canvas. Therefore for the new icon what is significant is not the color of the square but simply the fact of the cut out, that is the apophatic moment, about which I will have more to say later.

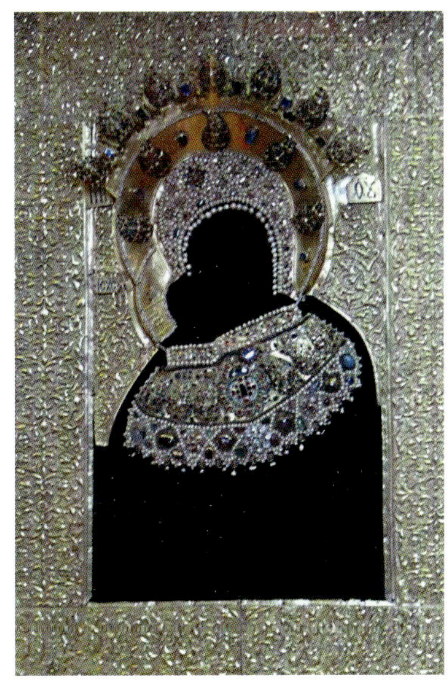

Riza *Our Lady Vladimirskaya*, Russian icon, silver, semi-precious stones,1686 State Historic Museum, Moscow Kremlin Workshops. The contribution of the Tsar Ioan Alekseevich, Peter the Great and Sophia to Alexander Uspensky Monastery

And one other thing. About gold and color, and about the *White Square* or the white canvas as a full-fledged substitute for the gold frame. What follows are the thoughts of the contemporary French historian Michel Pastoureau:

Gold in reality presents an ethical problem. As a color, it equates with the divine: noble gold. But as material object it symbolizes earthly wealth, luxury, greed—*vanitas*. In addition, in gold, which is also a color, there is a maximum intensity of hue, which means there is a moral problem linked to the concentration of color, which we spoke of earlier. This can be used, perhaps, to create a hierarchy of values: gold, which in the medieval mind and culture had little in common with the color yellow, was in fact tightly linked to the color white and was sometimes used to express the concept of pure whiteness, hyper white: this chromatic gradation was sometimes necessary to emphasize the hierarchical superiority of the heavenly or divine (the world of angels, for example), but neither the lexicon nor artistic practice was capable of adequately capturing it given the relatively narrow spectrum of available white tones. *In the Middle Ages, gold was whiter than the whitest white.*[1] (my emphasis)

(See, for example, the white gold in Igor and Marina's painting *Seven Brides*, 2012)

Queen Elizabeth I and Pinturicchio: Bas relief, Silhouette and Frame
A few works in this album are in direct dialogue with the genre of the silhouette and also with Malevich's tradition of the new icon: specifically *Copper Queen* (2007) and *One and a Half Boys in Red* (2007).

In order to appreciate how our two artists understand the concept of the new icon and why they do so, we need to ask: what is an icon in the contemporary world anyway? Is it a religious object or an art object (after all, icons were never traditionally art objects)? The position of the non-Orthodox majority, even without any attempt at aesthetic argumentation, would be the latter (they would likely see the religious, but first and foremost [for them] paintings of Giotto or Rafael in the same way). And in that case, if we take the argument a bit farther, the religious subject of the icon, its center (let us say the depicted saint or the Holy Savior) becomes almost the same kind of aesthetic phenomenon as a tiger or a diamond. It is beautiful, they will say, and that is all there is to it. That is, no explanation is required. Since even in "simply beautiful" there is a kind of sacred secret, something mystical.

In Malevich's new icon we find all the elements of old art save one—the figure (although, by the way, in a traditional icon the concept of figure is a relative one since there can be no quotidian forms in the non-material world). That is why it remained in the realm not only of the museum but also of pure metaphysics. It was non-art that thought up the secular icon: a soup can, Elizabeth Taylor, and Mao are completely equivalent, that is artistically identical in such icons and are therefore not sacred in any way (the spiritual world preserves the concept of hierarchy), but are simply someone's personal objects of devotion. And this list, in contemporary art, can be expanded endlessly.

However the secular icon can also be something entirely different. After all, the subject of a traditional religious icon is not only an image known to everyone (canonized), but a face or faces that have an absolutely equal value (meaning) to absolutely everyone, which simply cannot be said about Mao, or even Jasper Johns' "American Flag", despite the adjective "pop" often appended to this type of art. And, paradoxical as this may sound now, traditional icons were for a long time in all of Western civilization carriers of equal meaning for all, since non-believers simply did not exist, and in the Islamic and Jewish traditions depictions of faces were prohibited.

And this "immutable rock of values" (in Osip Mandelstam's words), that is, this unchangeable, like a rock, hierarchy, specifically in "icon art" must continue to exist, at least formally, even when an icon becomes a secular object. After all, an icon has to be worshipped, as a (global) sacred object, even if it is one that has not necessarily been placed on the UNESCO list.

Of course, in today's postmodern culture a teddy bear and the Mona Lisa are equal as subjects, but in the hierarchy of everyone's values they will never be equal, in just the same way that Leonardo or Elizabeth I or Suleiman the Magnificent can easily become characters in popular computer games (and have already done so) but remain irreplaceable as cultural figures because they are not doubted: no one else can take their place in the broad cultural memory.

Similarly, in addition to historical personages there are also many artistic images (or literary ones) that can (or already have) become irreplaceable figures, sacralized by our general cultural memory or their museum/auction status.

In the context of any culture, secular art is merely a continuation of religious art. Every icon is simply sacred. In this sense the jewels in its frame—if they are or ever were there—are merely tautologic in relation to its basic mystic reality. But a painting becomes valuable (or invaluable) in the eyes of others, that is, normal people, only if it enters the Louvre or the Guggenheim or some other prestigious collection or artistic album: until that point it has value only for the artist (and of course, for the angels, who look at all of human history from above, from the world of truly absolute values).

Here we have to take into account the fact that the western Catholic world, as opposed to the Orthodox countries, did not have much contact with the culture of the icon as such. Icons and wall painting, including mosaics there, beginning with the schism of the one Christian church in the eleventh century, were gradually replaced by religious paintings and frescoes (while in the later Protestant world, as is well known, the domains of the church and of visible art were generally incompatible).

This is why Igor & Marina choose as the subjects of their new, secular icons those images which are generally recognized (and therefore instantly legible to all) in our post-confessional and globalized world. And the frame for their secular icons becomes that which is usually called the background of the painting.

To qualify what I have said immediately, although I will return to the philosophical background in the pictures of Igor & Marina more than once, it is worth noting that the largest group of paintings in this album is comprised of works in which the background (frame, clothing) serves as an ornament, and the figures (and faces) seem to be cut out of that ornament. The background can be:

- an imaginative design of a rug, as in the paintings *Big Infanta* (2005), *Harvest Moon* (2007), *Africa* (2009) or *The Color of Pomegranates* (2010);

- some kind of tile or wallpaper that could be called William Morrisesque, as in the paintings *Air of Time* (2003) or *To the Tips of Her Nails* (2005);

- the background ornament appearing as an enormous costume, as for example in *Secrets of the Madrid Court* (2006) or *Triple Life of Elizabeth* (2004);

- it can even show up as an elemental decoration, as in the painting *Angels Normally Don't Fly When It's Raining* (2005).

Even if I were to try, in this short essay I could not paraphrase all of the ornamental designs of Igor & Marina or even partially explain their multitudinous meanings. Therefore I would like to concentrate on just a few paintings in which the frame

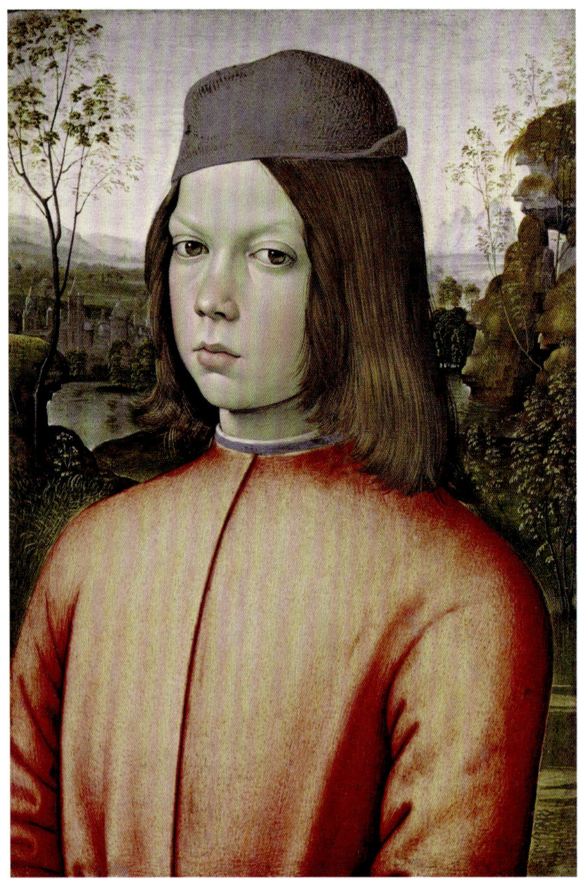

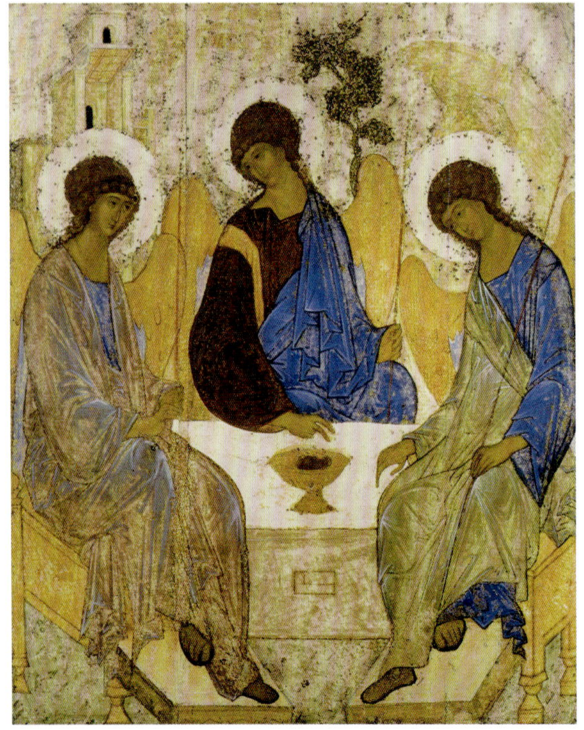

Pinturicchio, *Portrait of a Boy*, c. 1500
Dresden, Gemäldegalerie Alte Meister,
Staatliche Kunstsammlungen

Andrei Rublev, *The Trinity*, 1420–30
Moscow, The State Tretyakov Gallery

is more metaphysical than ornamental; that is, where it exhibits a metaphorical richness that engenders a narrative.

In contrast to the kind of ornamented space that is typical for any well decorated icon frame, the background to the diptych entitled *Copper Queen* (2007) is of a uniform, very deep "cognac" color. This makes sense: Queen Elizabeth I was known for her deep red hair. But this is merely the first key to the background color. That is, it becomes a key only when we look at the right side of the diptych, a stylized official-style portrait *en face* (or in half profile) of the Virgin Queen in red tones; her hair, eyes, clothes and the painting's background are linked through this reddish color scale — in all of its subtle variations — which is almost a form of *grisaille*.

But if we look at the left side of the diptych, we see, in place of a detailed portrait of the queen, an <u>absence</u>. To be more accurate, now we see, as if cut out of a piece of metal (and following exactly the contours of the image on the right side), a silhouette: a reddish space.

In other words, the left side of the diptych has become, quite literally, a metal frame for the right — painted — side. We see a new type of secular icon, preserving all the formal features of the two-piece traditional icon (the board and the frame). It is as if the artists are showing us how an icon is made; they are laying bare the device (to use the term of the Russian formalists) at the level of both craft and symbolism.

In the painting *One and a Half Boys in Red* (2007) it would seem that we have exactly the same compositional principle, only presented in a much more complicated fashion. In the center of the painting we see three portraits of a boy, one of which (on the far left) is almost a perfect replica of the famous *Ritratto di un ragazzo*, 1500) of Pinturicchio (1454–1513), which currently hangs in the Old Masters Museum in Dresden.

What is more, the portrait is also *en face* (or in half profile) as was that of Queen Elizabeth in the painting discussed above. However, the second portrait of the boy, in the center, is not as complete as the first one (the one on the left); only the boy's face has been fully painted, while his hat and all of his clothing have been replaced by white emptiness which, if we recall the words of Michel Pastoureau, is equivalent to the meaning of gold in the art of the middle ages.

In the third portrait of the boy, the interior of the far right painting, the face (in addition to the hat and clothing) has also become a white silhouette outline: thus, the painted portrait completely disappears in the white contours that have been reproduced on the canvas.

If one knows nothing about the traditional icon, the philosophical meaning of this progression disappears and all one sees is a kind of painterly paraphrase of the famous cry of Maksim Gorky's hero Klim Samgin (which long ago became a Russian catch phrase): "Did that boy ever exist?" (Russians use this phrase when they want to express doubt that something actually happened).

This painting, however, depicts a real philosophical event, which in theology is linked most of all to the formula of the Holy Trinity, and is best known in the Russian tradition through Andrei Rublev's famous icon *Old Testament Trinity* (beginning of the fifteenth century, now in the Tretyakov Gallery in Moscow, see bottom left), which depicts three beautiful angel-youths sitting at a table on which there is a single goblet (in applied religious art this Trinitarian formula would become an actual form—the folding triptych icon).

Pinturicchio's fully angelic boy in Igor & Marina's painting is not so much a variation on the Dresden painting but more a development of Rublev's artistic idea of the Holy Trinity.

Specifically, following Rublev, the thought that the three angels (three hypostases of God) are similar and equally beautiful, contains within itself (the idea is, as it were, dissolved into the picture) the theological argument regarding *filioque* between the Christianity (that would be called Orthodoxy) of the Roman Eastern Empire and Western Christianity (Catholicism) that led to the great schism between the churches in the eleventh century.[2]

Igor & Marina's painting does not discuss the issue of what is the icon and what is the frame but rather whether the border between them—as between the hypostases of the Trinity—is a product of thought (rational) or remains completely intuitive (personal, emotional).

To put it more simply: just as a person's shadow (silhouette) depends not on the person himself but on the sun, so the hierarchy of the beautiful depends on a higher authority than us.

At the same time, however, we need to keep in mind that in Igor & Marina's painting the right side acts as the frame for the whole left side while the central section (that is, the part which shows only the boy's face) exists here like the face of an icon seen in the cut out space provided by the frame.

In other words, that which in the icon is seen as a sum, that is, what we see at the same time and in 3D, laid one atop the other (the board + the image [with its layers of paint and colors] + the frame with its openings for the image[s]), has been carefully dismantled here, divided into three dimensions but exhibited on a single plane—the canvas.

Background as Narrative
The philosophy of the background in the work of Igor & Marina is by no means limited to the formal and conceptual specifics of the icon.

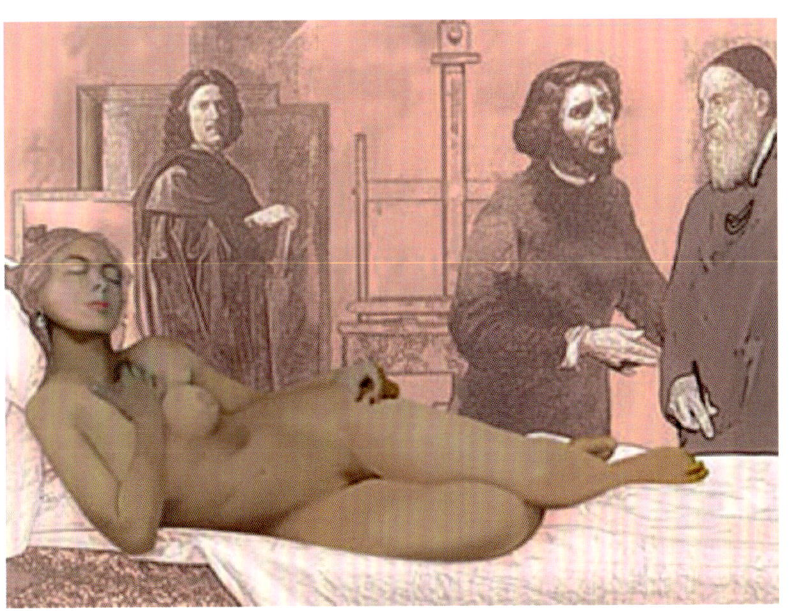

In order to explain the method of analysis that I will now use to understand the work of Igor & Marina and to show how their work fits into the context of contemporary world art (and is not an exception to it), it seems crucial to turn to an example from Western art, and particularly to one of its most important contemporary works.

I have in mind *Balzac,* the last work (unfinished but already famous, see bottom left) of Richard Hamilton (1922–2011).

One could say that the background of this painting, which was first called *The Unknown Masterpiece*, just like the story by Balzac, follows the spirit of *grisaille* (recall *Copper Queen*), and that the figures in the back are simply part of the background pattern (the ornament) since they are rosy reflections (or shadows) of the sepia in which the figure in the front section of the painting is drawn. As a result, we could argue that the viewer does not need to recognize them, despite the fact that these are images of famous artists who are well known from their (self)portraits: from the left they are Poussin, Courbet, and Titian.

Hamilton, like Igor & Marina, is not ashamed of his citationality (without which postmodern art is impossible in any case) since it is not a question of borrowing (influence) but rather citationality as an artistic meaning-generating agent.

Although we are not supposed to recognize the concrete source (the literal source) of the naked model in the foreground, she is simultaneously a "child of photorealism" (or of "photoshop") and from the same pleiad as, for example, Giorgione's Venus or the works of Titian recalled by his presence in the background: here, for example is his *Venus of Urbino* (1538, top right)).

But what is more important in Hamilton's painting, the model or the background? The model is what we notice first, and the figures of the artists, only later, and the question, who are these guys? comes up still later. So we might say that obviously the model is the most important thing. Because "she is beautiful!" and so on, while the figures of the artists fill, for us, the same kind of *landscape function* as, for example, the trees, hills and sky in Renaissance paintings of nudes, such as, for example, in Giorgione's *Sleeping Venus* (1505–10, bottom right).

Nevertheless, in Hamilton's painting the figures are of specific artists, which implies that these artists in particular and not some other ones mean something. It is not for nothing that there are exactly three of them, like Rublev's angels or Igor & Marina's boys, and not a whole crowd, as, for example, the doctors in Rembrandt's painting who surround a naked corpse in a morgue wearing their solemn Dutch costumes. Let us look more closely: the three figures exist in a kind of twilight, like background trees and sky. And even more interesting, they are like photographs in a dark room, where photos are developed and printed.

If we don't know who these figures are, then the story that the background tells us is a fairy tale about a photographic Galatea, some kind of photo-nymph who became real flesh, and who made the three creators fall in love with her. Or got them to fight over her. Or she became a sleeping beauty waiting for another prince (of course, I will not attempt to narrate all the possible stories here).

But if we know that these images are of Poussin, Courbet, and Titian, then we might see a different story: about the twilight of old art and the equal greatness of new art, which cannot exist without the aesthetics of photorealism and pin-up girls.

The background of Hamilton's painting is not even a key to it, but is that which allows for the possibility of narrative. That is, the background is what the painting is about, its central intellectual and emotional subject.

The Background as the Depiction of an Absence
At the same time, the background of Hamilton's picture is also that which is not mentioned there; that is, it includes within it that which is absent in the background: a depiction (portrait), of the artist Giorgione, for example.

After all, Hamilton's model (she is according to Hamilton, *The Unknown Masterpiece* of Balzac) is formally much closer to Giorgione's Venus than she is to Titian's; in the former's work she is precisely sleeping and not simply recumbent and wide awake, as in the *Urbino Venus*. But since we already know about the invisible presence of Giorgione (he is there, invisibly present), there is no need to draw his fig-

Titian, *Venus of Urbino*, 1538
Florence, Galleria degli Uffizi

Giorgione, *Sleeping Venus*, 1508–10
Dresden, Gemäldegalerie Alte Meister,
Staatliche Kunstsammlungen

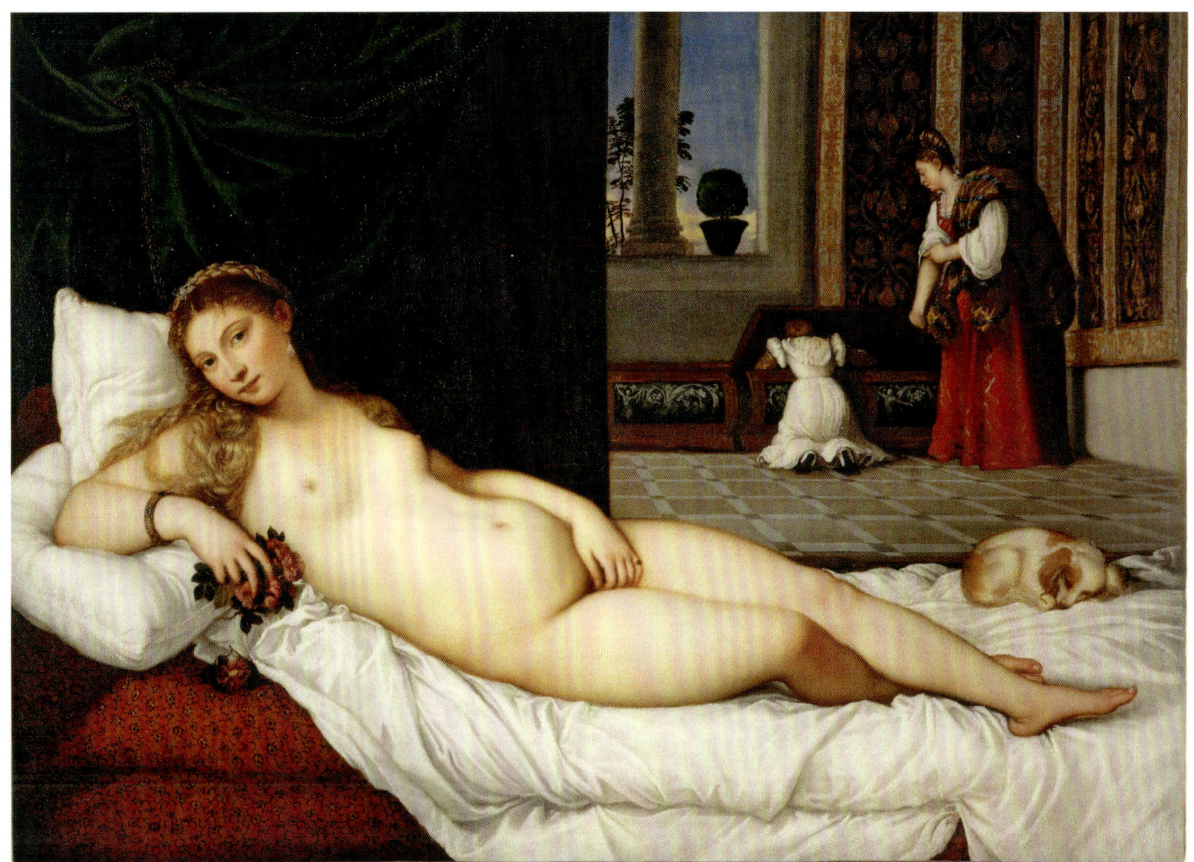

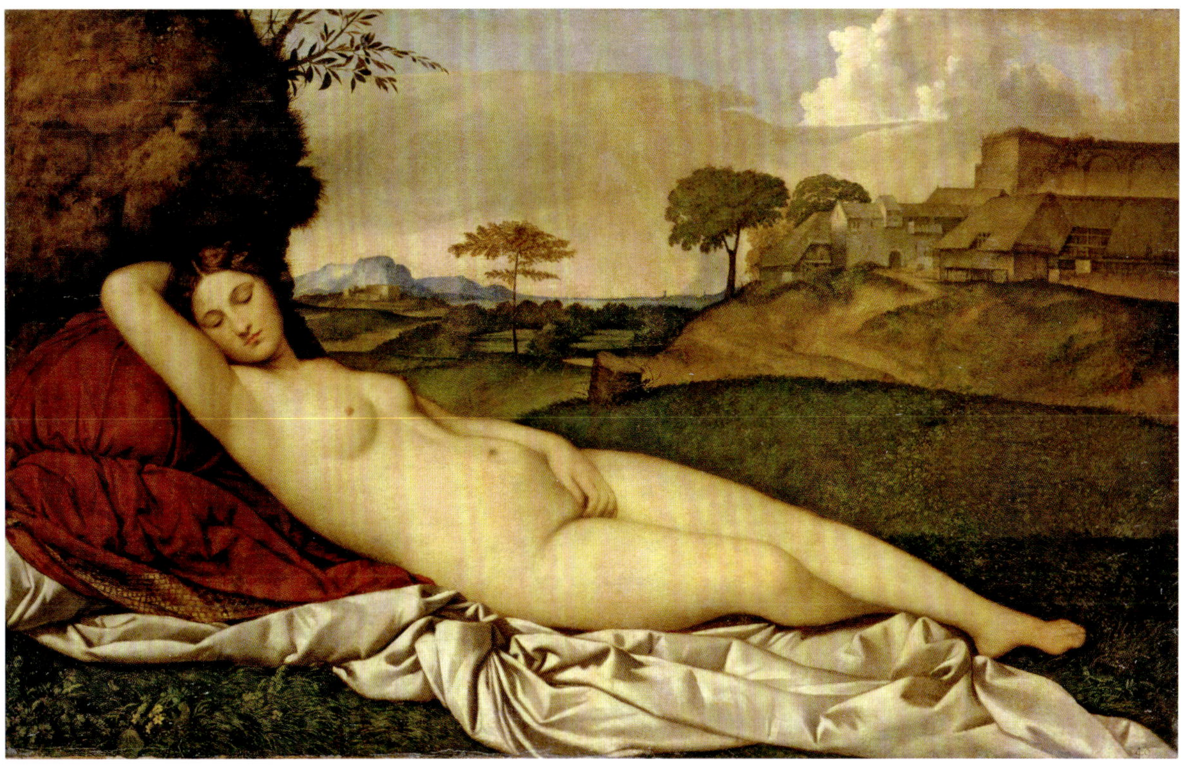

ure in, just as it is unnecessary to include Goya (with his overly famous *Naked Maja*) or Edouard Manet (with his overly scandalous *Olympia*).

The presence of Poussin in Hamilton's painting is motivated more phonetically than visually, although Poussin also has some sleeping Venuses (*Sleeping Venus and Cupid*, around 1630, or *Sleeping Venus Surprised by Satyr*, 1626). To be sure, however, these paintings can in no way compete in terms of popularity with *Maja* or *Olympia*, but Poussin's name, for the British Hamilton, cannot help but be suggestively connected to the semi-obscene word *pussy*.

In this way, the background of the painting takes into account through visual association that which is not present (although it really is, perhaps?) — and the whole obscene situation (look at the arrangement of the figures on the canvas) here is quite similar to the frequently used artistic subject of *Susanna and the Elders* drawn from the Biblical *Book of Daniel*; and Giorgione is there, as are Goya and Manet.

In theology, philosophy and aesthetics, this type of thinking is called apophatic.[3] Precisely apophaticism as the depiction of the absent is one of the central aesthetic (and ethical) themes of Igor & Marina's painting: the invisible exists.

For starters, let's return to the painting *One and a Half Boys in Red* which I have already discussed extensively in connection with the aesthetics of the icon and which makes use of Pinturicchio's *Portrait of a Boy*.

In Pinturicchio, beyond the shoulders of the boy (see the illustration above) we can see (fairly far away, but quite clearly) water and trees and then, even farther away, hills, the whole traditional array of objects for the background of a Renaissance painting (see, for example, the *Mona Lisa* or Giorgione's *Sleeping Venus*).

In Igor & Marina's painting, beyond the shoulders of the boy (of whom we see three, not one) we appear to glimpse the same landscape, but that landscape is disappearing. We see the same water, trees and hills but almost as if through the window of a speeding train, and therefore washed out, like in a water color or a photograph that is out of focus (the boy is in focus, the landscape, not).

Furthermore, the more the boy begins to disappear, the more washed out the landscape beyond his shoulders becomes; the landscape, like the boy, becomes more and more absent, although his silhouette, as I said earlier, remains, as do the signs of the disappeared landscape, moving from left to right.

In other words, the materiality of both gradually disappears, becoming a silhouette or an outline, transparent or even a transparency. The border between presence and absence becomes the same as between existing and invisible: that is, conventional in the purest sense of the word.

But that is not all, as I have only written about the central section of Igor & Marina's painting, which is actually comprised of three horizontal planes.

On the upper plane, where there are no figures at all and where there seems, for those who do not know Russian, to be merely a gray and white (or whitish gray) abstract pattern, there are nevertheless words depicted (yes, depicted and not merely written!) in the Cyrillic alphabet — Элигических затей (of elegiac play — yes, just like that, with a capital letter and in the genitive case).

These words will doubtlessly confuse anyone who does not realize that they have been ripped out of the context of the first strophe of a famous poem that Anna Akhmatova (1889–1966) wrote in 1940: "Мне ни к чему одические рати/И прелесть элегических затей./По мне, в стихах всё быть должно некстати./Не так, как у людей." (I have no need of odic hosts/nor the charm of elegiac play./Poems for me must be outrageous/not at all the normal way). And even more, the rest of the poem (two more strophes) are inscribed in very small script in the same plane, with the exception of one word—окрик (shout) which is drawn in the same cursive but in much bigger letters (the same size used for the words *Elegiac play* and ripped out of the final strophe: "Сердитый окрик, дегтя запах свежий,/Таинственная плесень на стене…/И стих уже звучит, задорен, нежен,/На радость вам и мне." (An angry shout, the smell of fresh-lain tar,/Mysterious mold along the wall…/A poem's already coming, tender, lively/to your and my delight.)

Thus, from Akhmatova's poem the artists have emphasized three words which when combined create a completely new thought: Элегических затей окрик ("Elegiac play's shout"), that it is a new and independent phrase in the painting can be seen by the fact that it begins, according to proper orthographic rules, with a capital letter.

We need to recall here that at the foundation of any elegy is the feeling of loss. An elegy is always written about something that was but that is no more. That is why the meaning of Akhmatova's poem (which is about from what and how poems arise within her) changes to Igor & Marina's fascinating statement: precisely loss cries out in human beings, angrily pulls at human beings (and their individual life force); loss is precisely the cry of life that causes a person to pause, stop, and then freeze, if only for a moment.

So it turns out that the gradual disappearance of the boy (in the middle plane of the picture) and the disappearance (but at a different speed) of the landscape beyond his shoulders was already prefigured in the first (upper) part of the panel, and that the entire painting is a kind of painterly elegy for Pinturicchio's boy (and therefore, in terms of genre connected not only to the icon, as we have already demonstrated, but also to the famous Fayum funerary portraits).[4]

The third, lower panel of the painting serves as an interpretation or a summing up of the other two parts: here we no longer have the grayish white (or whitish gray) abstraction (apparent abstraction) of the upper panel, but rather we see white and leafless trees against a gray black background (either a mountain or the night sky). Most important, there are precisely three trees, and each of them is placed directly below one of the portraits of the boy. If we don't know what the upper part of the painting is talking about (loss), then the upper and lower sections seem merely to be artistic frames surrounding the central (portrait) section. That is, they seem there to create a strong visual effect and nothing more.

If we understand that the whole picture is also an elegy, then the leafless trees (in their winter phase) on the lower panel (section)—fit perfectly into the genre of loss.

But that is not all, because the lower part of the painting looks, in fact, like a photographic negative, that is an undeveloped photograph. If we keep in mind the photographic trick in the central part of the painting (recall the landscape beyond the boy's shoulders), then the disappearance of his image is summed up in the lower panel by a kind of deep mourning for him. We see not only a colored obituary and not only a landscape necropolis (the leafless trees which look like standing gravestones), but a new apophatic statement: a negative (in of itself) is that which is not, precisely because that which is, is hidden, or not (yet) developed.

And let us not forget that the themes of photography and the photographic laboratory are present in Hamilton's painting and add a lot to its meaning.

The Depiction of the Absent as a Catalogue
And now let us turn to some other paintings by Igor & Marina in which the so-called

absent is not merely a sign of its actual presence, but in which it becomes a kind of apophatic catalogue.

The catalogue is one of the central epic devices in art (especially in literature); it should be sufficient to recall the famous "list of ships" in Homer's *Iliad*, in which the author tots up (and describes) each one of the thousand or so Achaean ships (if we wish to correct Marlowe's formula of "a thousand ships" we might note that there were actually a few more: 1186), that set off to win back Helen and conquer Troy; and if we recall that in this list, in addition to the names of the ships, Homer also gives us the names of the captain of each one, that is, the future heroes of the war itself, then we can appreciate why the Homeric catalogue is so extensive.

We can also say that if the catalogue (then) was a case of overwrought detalization, the exaggerated piling on of details (specificities) and then in the visual arts its apogee occurred during the Baroque period, as illustrated by the works of Rubens, for example. But the works of Homer, and of Rubens, and the stone sculptures of Notre Dame Cathedral all express the same thing—that the world is infinite, that there is and can be no end to its details, that the epic—like the catalogue (or the list) is always potentially endless, without end or even beginning: it can start anywhere and end anywhere as well. In just the same way, for example, striving to the heights cannot end, even in the case of a Gothic cathedral like Notre Dame; it was built over the course of some 200 years, and eventually the building stopped where it stopped because it is impossible to touch God.

From all of this, we can see that any catalogue, even the longest, is just a small fragment of the eternal, but at the same time it is a fragment which can only be completed if we provide some artificial parameters: describe, for example only 9 or 50 of the final days of the Trojan War (according to other readings of the *Iliad* it is actually 10, 49 or 53), and not its entire lengthy and tragic decade: put together a list not of all of humanity starting with A and ending with Z but only, for example, the inhabitants of a single town, and even there, for example, limit yourself to those who have telephones.

But if it is impossible to draw, describe, or name absolutely everything that there is, then perhaps it is possible, in the same hapless way (only backwards), to try to name everything that there is not. Theologians (Parmenides, Plato, Dionysius the Areopagite, Plotinus, Thomas Aquinas) tell us that the absolute (God) is absolutely unknowable and, therefore, any list of his attributes, as, for example, his beauty or greatness, will nevertheless be just as incomplete as the list of our words to describe those aspects of his being which are totally unavailable to our understanding and therefore simply are absent as far as we are concerned.

But the list of "what we do not know about God" will also necessarily be incomplete. As a result, the existence of knowledge about him and the absence of knowledge about him are fully equivalent from the perspective of negative (apophatic) philosophy and theology.

In the painting *Sofa* (2012) we can see an example of Igor & Marina's apophatic catalogue, but one of a completely new type. To start, let us note that the painting consists of three connected canvases; that is, it uses the artists' favored artistic format: the triptych. But this painting is less a folding icon (regarding that type of work, see above) but rather it is based on the model and principle of the three-part mirror.

Of course, in a formal sense a tri-fold mirror and a religious triptych have a lot in common, but their content (purpose) is rather different; the latter is a kind of mirror of the Absolute, which can be seen in it, while the former provides a reflection, simultaneously in all three mirrors, of a person him or herself. A person looking into a tri-fold mirror sees him or herself "in three faces." The middle part of the mirror, the largest, shows the person as he or she "is"; the right and left sides, assuming that we fold the mirror toward the center, cover, or better, obscure the middle part completely; that is, each of them, at least in size, makes up half of the center mirror; in them any person, squinting a bit, can see him or herself a bit differently than in the center mirror, since the two sides alter the reflection a bit.

In a tri-fold mirror, no matter how blasphemous this might sound at first blush, a person becomes the Trinity; although if we recall the Biblical claim that humans are made in the image and likeness of God, then the appearance of a person as three in one in a tri-fold mirror can be seen as a kind of confirmation of the Biblical postulate.

Sofa shows us on its left and right sides (we will call them that), a naked girl sitting on a sofa. And, as is to be expected in a mirror reflection, on the left side she is leaning a bit to her right, while on the right side she leans a bit to the left, which allows us to recognize that we have here not only a painting but a variant of a tri-fold mirror. In the middle of the painting, however, the reflection of the girl is … absent, and in its place is an entire "catalogue of ships" (to use the Homeric term), a painted catalogue of various sofas, couches, love seats, and even a full-fledged chaise longue à la Ingres. Why? And where did the girl go?

We recall that Igor & Marina's Pinturicchian boy also disappeared, but he did so gradually and at least he left behind a recognizable white silhouette.

Here, instead of a person's face we have sofas and couches and chaise longues. Now we have to remember that *Sofa* (the name of the painting) in Russian does not mean merely a particular piece of furniture, but is also a common diminutive of the woman's name Sophya or Sophia (Софья, София). In Russian, the stress on the two words differs; with the object the stress is on the first syllable and with the name on the last. In English, however, the two are stressed identically and the name of the painting is in English, not in Russian.

However, the painting is based not merely on a bilingual pun, but also on a very deep apophatic belief that a person is first and foremost a name.[5] It is not that a person has a name but rather than a concrete name defines the character and fate of the person.

In this way, the fact that the central portion of the painting reflects not the girl but her name and a catalogue of objects that are, in Russian, homographically and in English homonymically connected to her name makes the entire picture a visual philosophical generalization. Plus, we can ask ourselves the question: What remains after a person is gone? A body?—no, it turns to dust. A reflection?—obviously not. Then what?—precisely his or her name, which is also the basis of his or her life's work.

The apophatic catalogue also lies at the basis of the painting *Hold Tight & Carry On* (2012). This is not a three-part canvas, but is still a triptych of a certain kind. The painting is divided into three uneven horizontal pieces (panels): the top one is the medium sized one in terms of width, the central one is quite small, and the bottom one is by far the largest. However, we first pay attention to the middle, narrowest one (it is practically nothing but a stripe) because it <u>demands</u> our attention. As opposed to the top and bottom panels, which are divided into neat squares with an image in each one, the central section is bright red, like a red traffic light, which grabs our attention. And furthermore, this red stripe is a kind of iconic frame on which, as in the conventional cut out pieces or "windows" on an icon, we can see a women's hands. And these hands are "speaking", in the sense that they have been captured at a moment of heightened gesticulation against the red background.

Then we understand that these hands belong to three (again three) female figures, who are rendered in graphic contours and since the whole red stripe is very narrow, we only see the central section of each of them and our attention is focused on their hands. Now we recognize that each of the women is holding a purse. The women on the left and in the center are holding it by the handle, while the one on the right is pressing it to her body imitating the same tender and careful gesture typical of the way the Mother of God holds her infant to her breast in Orthodox icons.

Furthermore, if the women on the left and the center are speaking with their hands, one of which is occupied with the purse and its handle, then the woman on the right is holding what in English is called a pouch purse, a clutch or an evening bag to her chest. This is important because the purse looks a bit like a diapered infant and the differences between these two kinds of bags are quite obvious.

Thus, in this painting we are not seeing one woman in three hypostases as was the case with, for example, the Pinturicchio boy in *One and a Half Boys in Red*, but rather three different women. What is important is that because the woman on the far right is not taking part in the dialogue of hands and is standing off by herself, the distance between her and the other two women, who are turned toward each other, is clearly larger than between the two of them. The woman on the right is completely separate, and we as viewers are likely therefore to think more about her than about, say, what the two other women are talking about in such a lively manner (also an interesting question, by the way).

Now let us have a look at the catalogue of purses shown in the neat squares in the painting's upper panel: there are 21 of them, seven in each of the three rows that make up the panel (in the lowest and biggest panel there are 35, as there are five rows in that panel). We won't spend our time on numerology, although of course any viewer is free to engage in extracting extra meaning from such facts just as he is in wondering why there are 1186 ships in Homer's catalogue and not a nice round number like Marlowe's 1000; or why the epic chooses to depict precisely 9, 20, 49, 51, or 53 days and not all ten years of the war. The number of purses in each part of the painting is not important in and of itself, but rather insofar as there are more (or less) in one part of the painting than in another.

Therefore we will regard the number of purses as a simple quantity: a simple fact about the visual catalogue (or the catalogues, as there are actually three of them). And since the catalogue is a visual one, it pays to look carefully and we see that not a single one of the purses in any of the squares is identical to any other one: they are all unique in terms of their design, color, material, and almost certainly their price, desirability and rarity.

It appears, then, that the purses are falling, almost like rain, from the top part of the painting down into the hands of the three women, but the purses that are in their hands do not correspond to any of the ones that are part of that purse "shower". Therefore we can assume that the purses in their hands are the result of a choice they made; and the bags that are continuing, as it were, to rain down from the top section of the painting to the bottom, passing right through the red stripe, only serve to confirm our timid hypothesis.

But why timid? Not at all. As one of the pillars of Plato's apophaticism asserted, there are many horses because there is really only one horse. He had in mind that the concept of the horse was materialized in their multiplicity; Parmenides, the father of negative philosophy, thought the same thing.

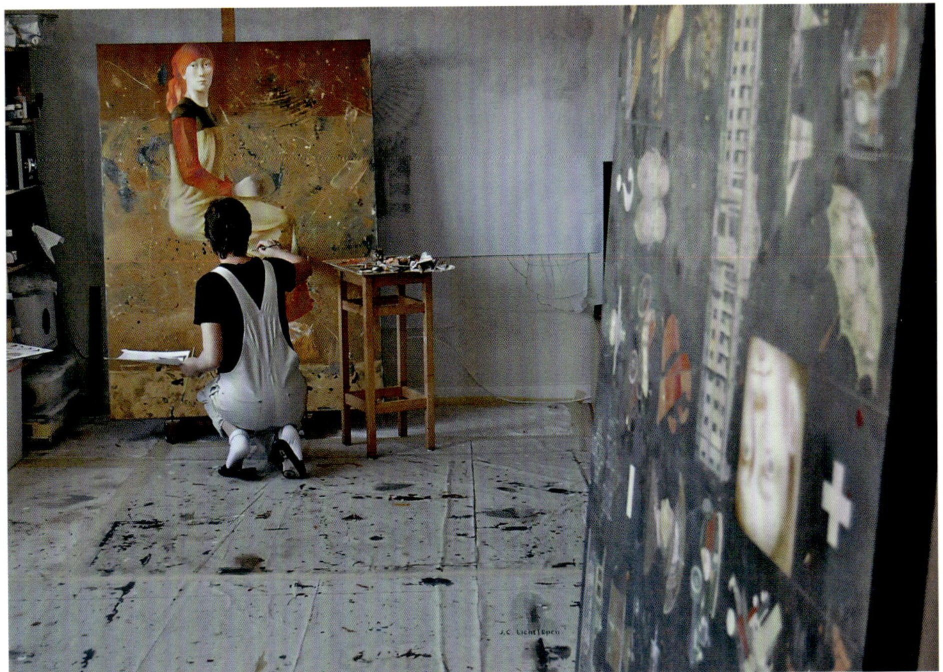

At the studio

(That the Platonic theme in Igor & Marina's painting is by no means accidental can be seen in their earlier work *Key Painting* [2008]. On the right side of this diptych we see a woman in a theatrical mask, who recalls Themis from the Empire Period, and who holds a key in each hand. And on the left side we see an enormous number of real metal keys, attached to a metal panel which is itself attached to a wooden board. I am sure that if this were not a diptych but a triptych, then on the far right side we would see St. Peter holding a single key, to the gates of heaven).

From the above it follows that one can easily interpret the catalogue of purses on the painting as pure apophaticism: that there is only a single concept of a purse, but that there are an endless number of purses; and that the women are choosing from this endless multitude which only gets larger and larger, as is shown by the lower panel of the painting. The moral of the story, for anyone who wants one, is that one should value one's own choice, particularly since it has already been made.

But at the same time, the woman who is pressing either a diapered baby or a vintage clutch (well yes, you can see the clasp) to her breast, is too individualized on the painting to limit her meaning to only a consumeristic choice. Any true artist is first and foremost a creature of association; if there is some kind of archetype "hanging" in his picture, then in his subconscious it must absolutely go off, like Chekhov's famous gun. If the clutch with its clasp in her hands looks like a baby, and the gesture with which she holds it recalls that of the Mother of God, then that means that the clutch (which is at the same time the Christ child and her own personal choice) is more elevated than a run-of-the-mill, quotidian purse. The rain of purses on the painting is at the same time the myth (that is, the archetype) of Danaë and the rain-Zeus which impregnated her and led to the birth of a demi-god; thus in the painting we also have the annunciation, immaculate conception, and the birth of the Son of God.

And in this case the separation of the woman on the right is far more meaningful than we thought up until now—she has chosen separation from the others: it is perhaps her mission and not a dead end of everyday over-production. Her choice is tragic and sacrificial, not at all consumeristic, because the last is always based on a desire to own and control, while the former two are not.

For lovers of numerology, I will just add that there are 59 purses in the picture while the Virgin lived for 72 years. The numbers don't coincide, but the archetypes do.

We turn now to the painting *Shoes, Legs... What Else* (2012), which in my view is the most obvious of Igor & Marina's catalogues. At first glance, it is organized according to the same logic as the previously discussed painting: here we see expressive female legs, there we found expressive female hands; here we see various women's shoes (sandals, short boots, and so forth), while there we saw various women's purses (clutches, pouch purses, handbags, and so forth). There, the first question was, what are the women holding in their hands? Clearly a purse. Here, for what are the women's legs "pining"? Clearly for wonderful high-heeled shoes. However, things are more complicated than they seem: psychologically the two situations are similar, but conceptually and philosophically, they are completely different.

The painting consists of two horizontal sections: in the one on top, the almost narrow one (later I will explain the "almost") there are five pairs of naked and unshod women's feet; in the lower, incomparably broader part of the canvas, occupying almost two thirds of the whole, there is a broad narrative catalogue of incredible female footwear from all epochs and of varied design, as if thought up precisely for the Shoe Museum in Toronto (the only one of its kind in the world, by the way).

At the same time, things are a bit more complex than they might seem at first glance because here what leads the parade, as it were, is precisely the color, which is what I am taking the risk of calling the background in this painting (that is the metaphysical *point* of the majority of Igor & Marina's works). The color of the background against which the shoes are exhibited recalls the heavy red velvet of the theatre curtain some kind of provincial pseudo-Moscow Art Theater (with all its worn out patches and holes) or, even more, the velvet insides of the sealed glass cases of some museum of fashion, or ethnography, with a subtle, almost colored light shining through, as is typical of museum displays.

Given that this part of the painting is the largest, then it is completely natural that specifically the color of the background against which the incredible quantity of women's footwear is displayed becomes a kind of curtain (to return to the previous metaphor) of a play (or more properly a pantomime) that our artists are acting out in front of our eyes. Look up quickly!—you see that the knees of all the sitting women are fastidiously covered in velvet of the exact same color and texture. This sharp color switch from the one that dominates the bottom part of the picture creates the sense that there are three parts to this painting, not two; that we, for the nth time in the work of Igor & Marina, are dealing with a triptych, not a diptych. I already referred to the work entitled *Key Painting* (2008), a diptych in which the third part needs to be intuited. That is speaking apophatically, it is already there, but the triptych has not yet been painted.

Here the equally elegant velvet of the dresses or skirts that links the knees of all the sitting women with its visual weight creates the highest—and almost completely independent—horizontal plane (panel) of the painting: it links (by covering them) specifically the knees and not the bare feet; while the feet, which stick out from under that theatrical velvet appear to be almost the porcelain—that is how white they are!—feet of marionettes or actresses who are acting in some kind of old fashioned absurdist play like *Les Chaises* by Eugene Ionesco; after all, it is clear that the women, sitting on these Ionescoesque chairs are playing some kind of absurd argument-conversation for the public in front of a partly lowered—that is, to the height of their knees, theatrical curtain.

Their faces and bodies are hidden behind this theatrical burka and as a result their words can definitely not be heard, and only their bare legs can be expressive, as in a *hamam*. That some kind of conversation is occurring can be intuited from the lower legs; the feet of one are straight, another one is rubbing one leg against another, a third one has her legs partially crossed, a fourth one has them in a kind of balletic position, while the fifth one's legs reveal that she is sitting partially facing the fourth one.

It becomes clear that the most important thing in the painting is not simply the dramaturgy, but the unusual approach of the director-metteur-en-scène (well yes, the directors, of course). And as a result, the rich shoe museum window, which takes up by far the largest amount of space in the picture, is not asking, for what are those women's feet pining (the answer is, "shoes, of course") but they are crying out about the nakedness of their feelings, about their bared souls (let us say). The entire relative nakedness of these legs (only from below the knee to the heel) grabs the viewer precisely because of their whiteness and defenselessness: they simply evoke a desire to cover them—that is, to defend them, put something on them, put them on heels, raise them up.

The apophaticism of this painted situation consists precisely in that very *else* that the painting itself asks us about (recall the name of the work); that which is in whatever quantity and assortment (shoes) is merely a pile of material, while the painting calls on us to turn our attention to something *else*, not in the sense of something different or absent but to the very existence of something beyond materiality yet present in nakedness and defenselessness; that is, to the soul of a human being, which, as opposed to various shoes, he or she, wears all through life, but which can neither be touched nor seen.

In just the same way we cannot know what makes a tree sad until the last leaf falls from it.

Literally a Few Words: Conclusion

In this essay, which has turned out a bit more poetic than I wanted it to be, it was most important for me to point out a few key themes, from a philosophical point of view, in the work of Igor & Marina, which stand out for their seriousness and consequentiality against the background of the worldwide fear about the disappearance of figurative art; this was more important to me than trying to go picture by picture through their work or, even worse, to attempt a chronological survey or to illustrate their various potential doubles in the past or present of the Russian artistic tradition.

I am sure that lovers of art and reviewers of this wonderful album will be able to find their way through Igor & Marina's other themes all by themselves.

[1] Michel Pastoureau. *Une Histoire Symbolique du Moyen Âge Occidental*. Paris: Éditions du Seuil, 2004. Cited from the Russian edition Символическая история Европейского Средневековья. Санкт-Петербург: Alexandria, 2012, c. 153–54.

[2] *Filioque* is a modification by the Catholic Church to the understanding of the Holy Trinity in the Nicene Creed, according to which the Holy Spirit does not proceed solely from God the Father, but from the Son as well. The Orthodox Church disagreed with this interpretation, citing the Holy Writ in which it is said that Jesus was baptized by the Holy Spirit. Thus, the question of *filioque* is a question regarding the hierarchy of the Trinity.

[3] On the sources of Orthodox apophatic thought and its meanings, see Timothy Ware. *The Orthodox Church*. London: Penguin Books, 1997, c. 63–4, 209.

[4] It is a curious fact that that the most famous of the approximately 900 Fayum portraits are held in Dresden's Staatliche Kunstsammlungen, which also holds Pinturicchio's *Portrait of a Boy*.

[5] On the influence of a name on the life and fate of a person, see Pavel Florensky, *Imena* (Moscow: Eksmo, 1998, pp. 449–522). Also see my essay *Stagnelius's Mustache* – Ilya Kutik. *Hieroglyphs of Another World*. Northwestern University Press, 2000, c. 87–104. It is also important to remember that Pavel Florensky (1882–1937) was also the author of perhaps the most famous philosophical tractatus devoted to the icon: *Iconostasis*.

ALL THE WORLD IS A STAGE SERIES

Newton's Law, study, pencil on paper,
68 × 72″ (173 × 183 cm)

Newton's Law, oil on canvas, 68 × 72″
(173 × 183 cm)

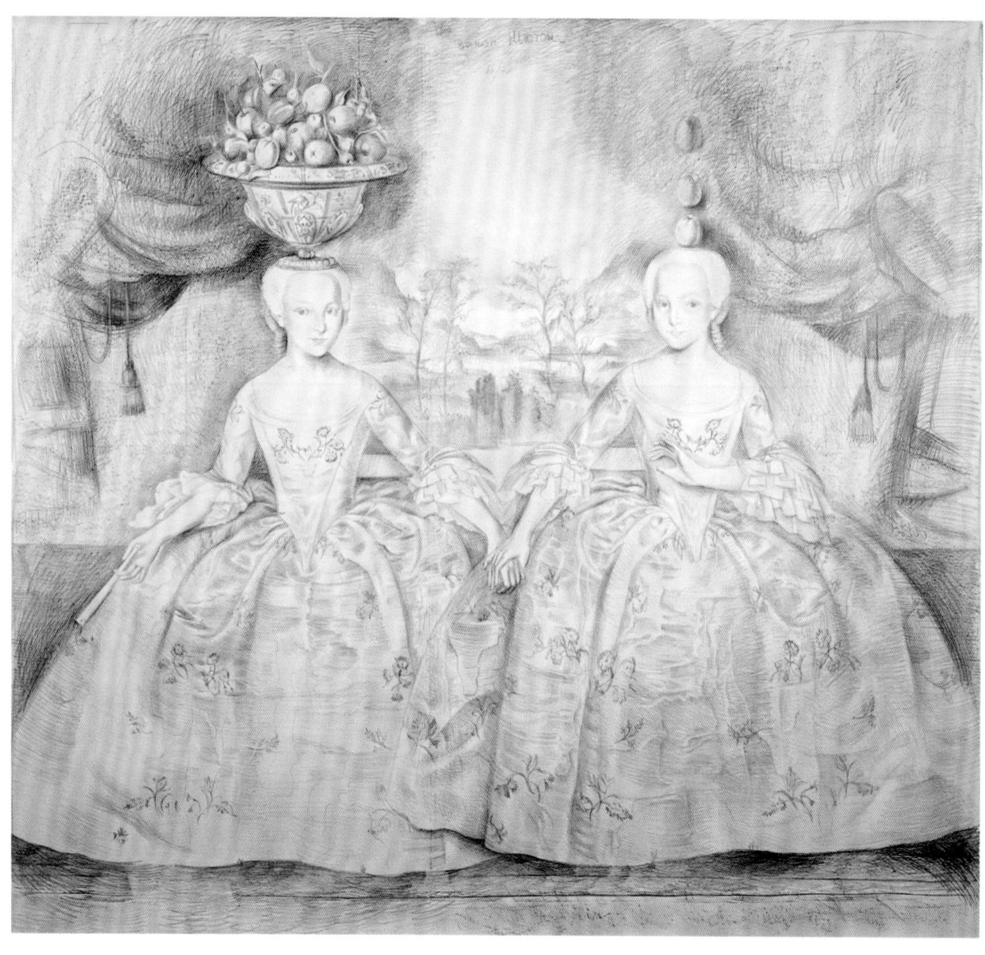

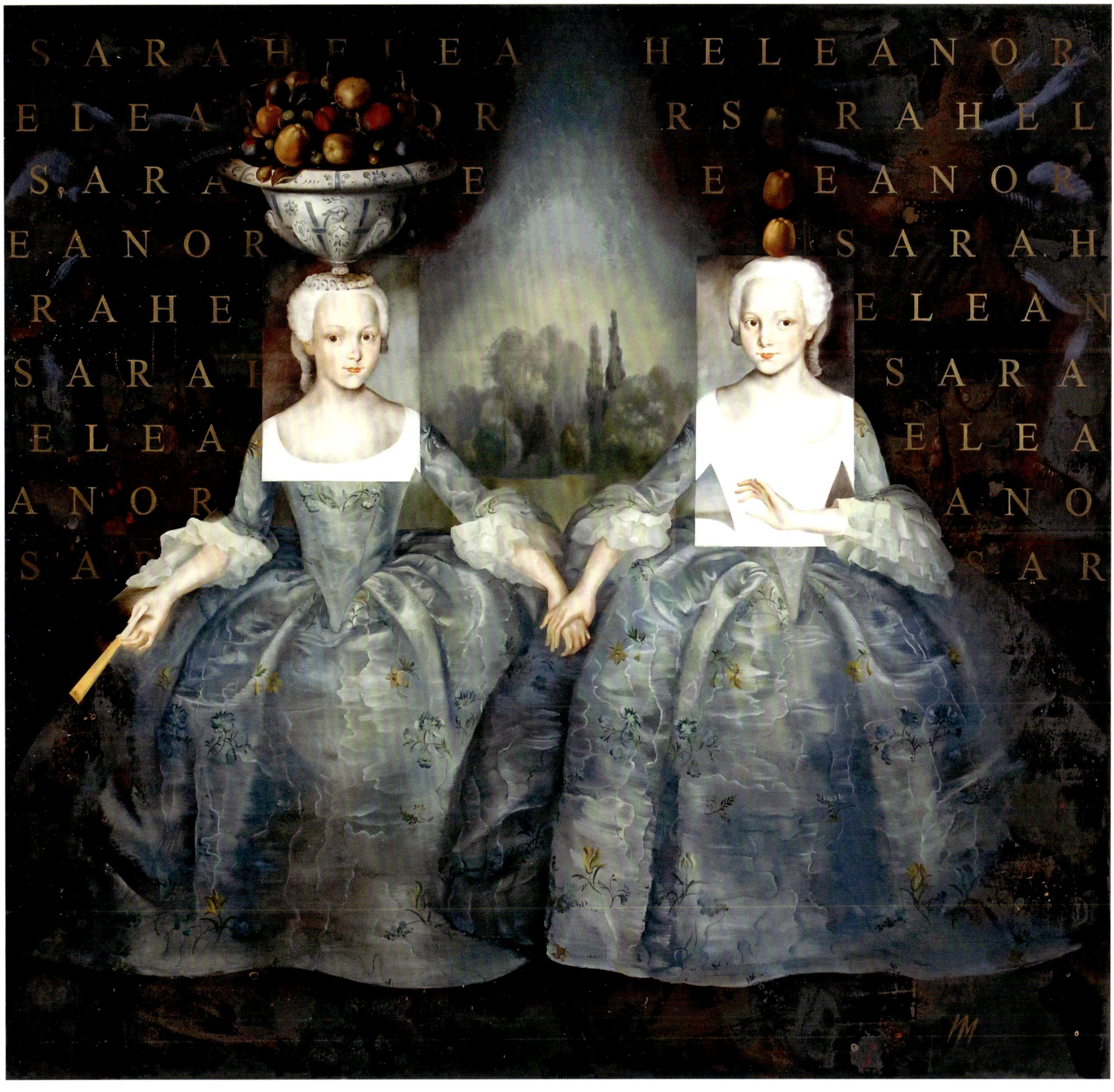

SARAH ELEA   HELEANOR
ELEA   OR   RS RAHEL
SARA   E   EANOR
EANOR   SARAH
RAHE   ELEAN
SARAI   SARA
ELEA   ELEA
ANOR   ANO
SAR   SAR

Commedia dell'Arte, oil on canvas, 40 × 60″
(102 × 152 cm)

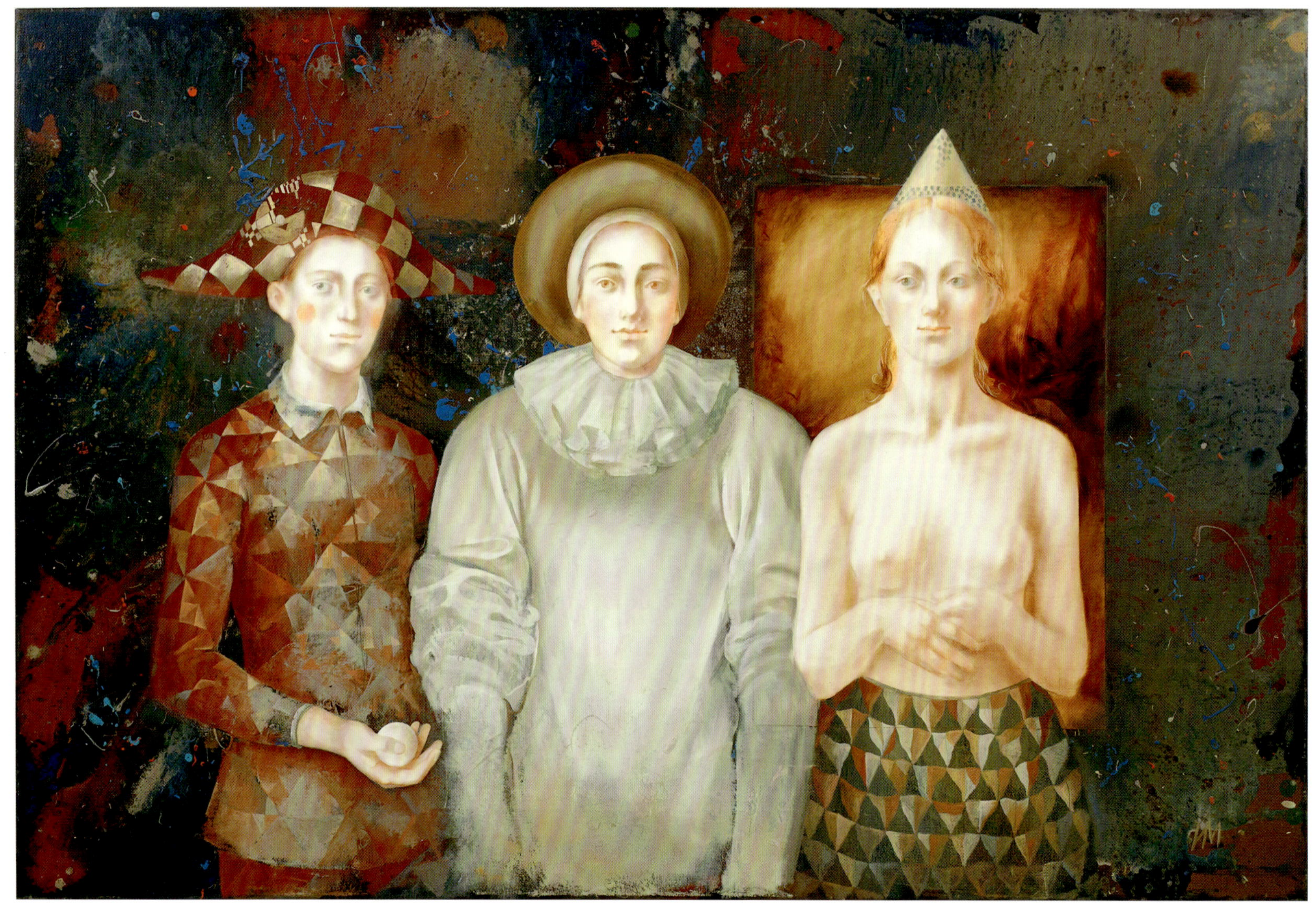

Good Morning, Maestro!, oil on canvas,
42 × 52″ (107 × 132 cm)

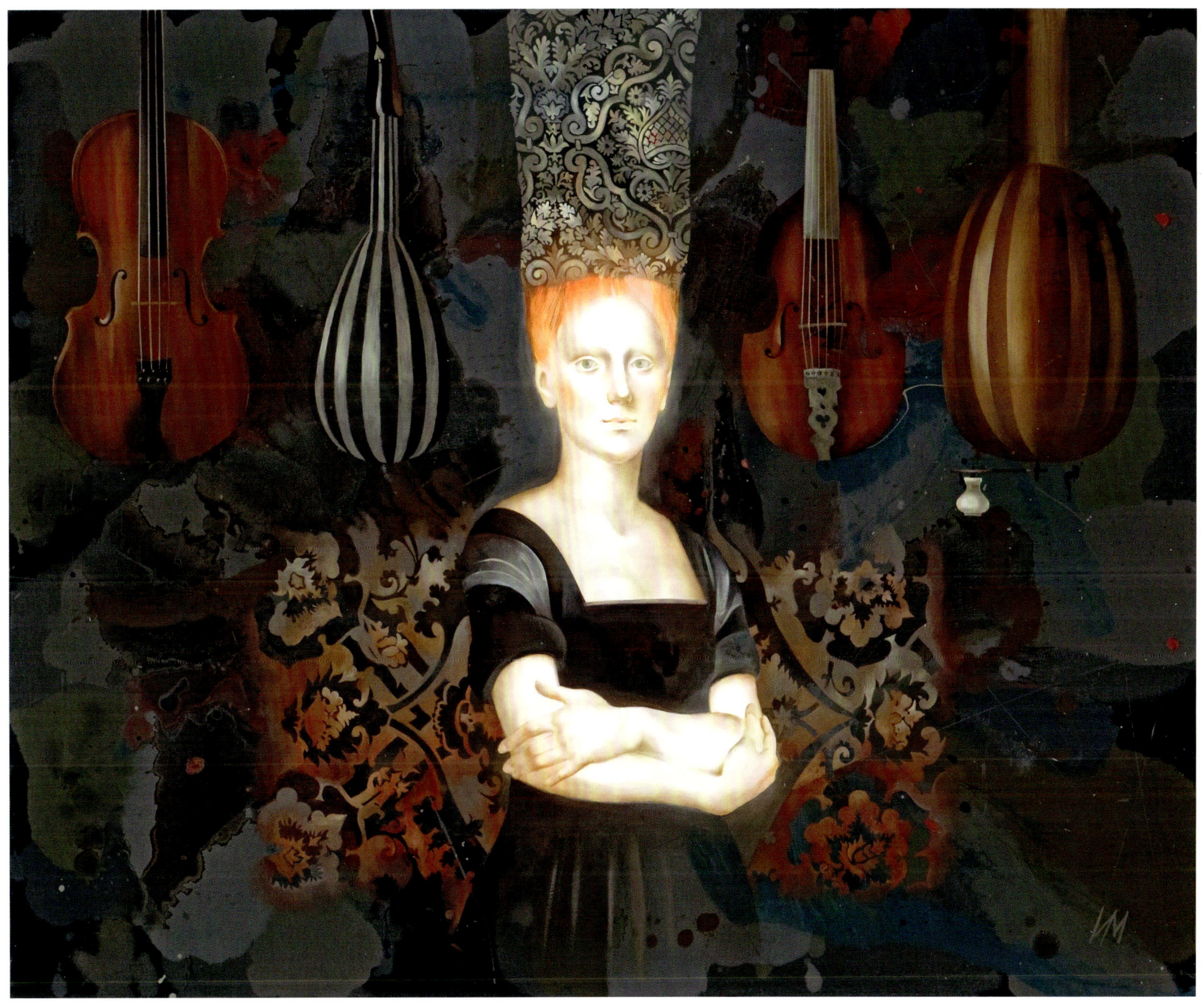

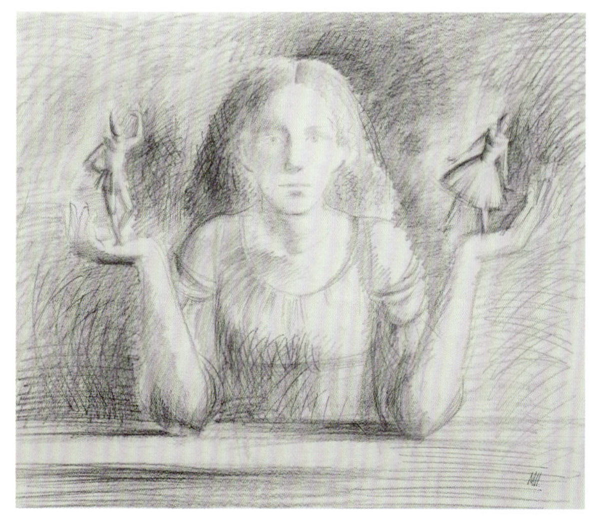

Little Dancers, study, pencil on paper,
30 × 40" (76 × 102 cm)

Little Dancers, oil on canvas, 32 × 42"
(81 × 107 cm)

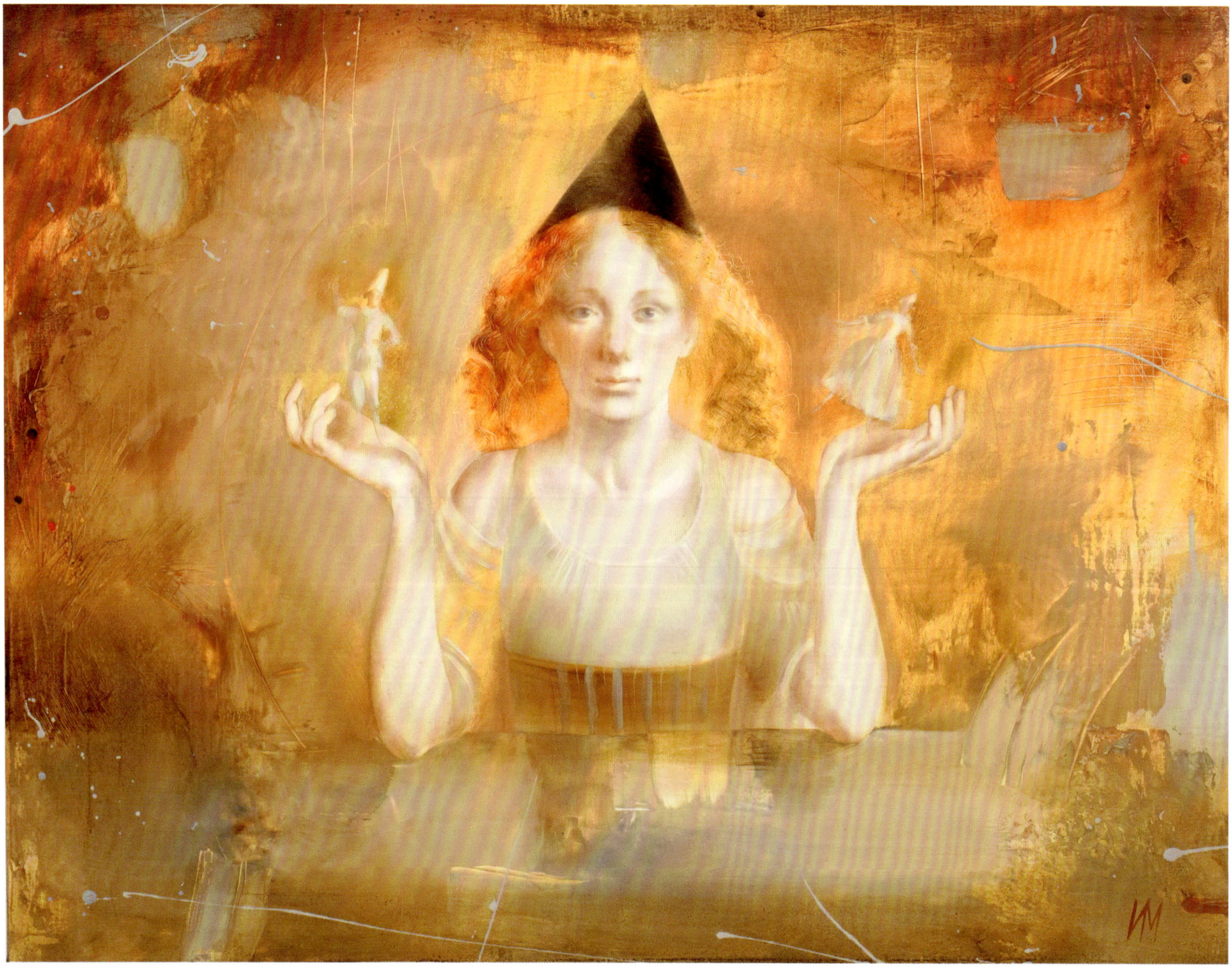

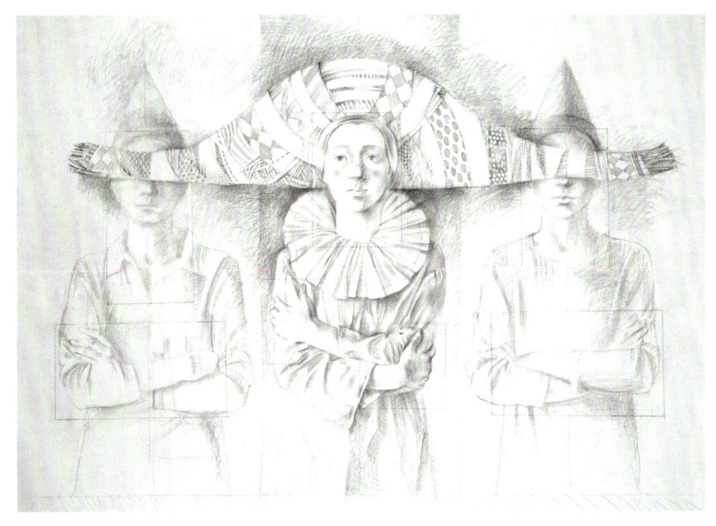

Napoleon, study, pencil on paper,
40 × 64″ (102 × 163 cm)

Napoleon, oil on Russian linen, 40 × 64″
(102 × 163 cm)

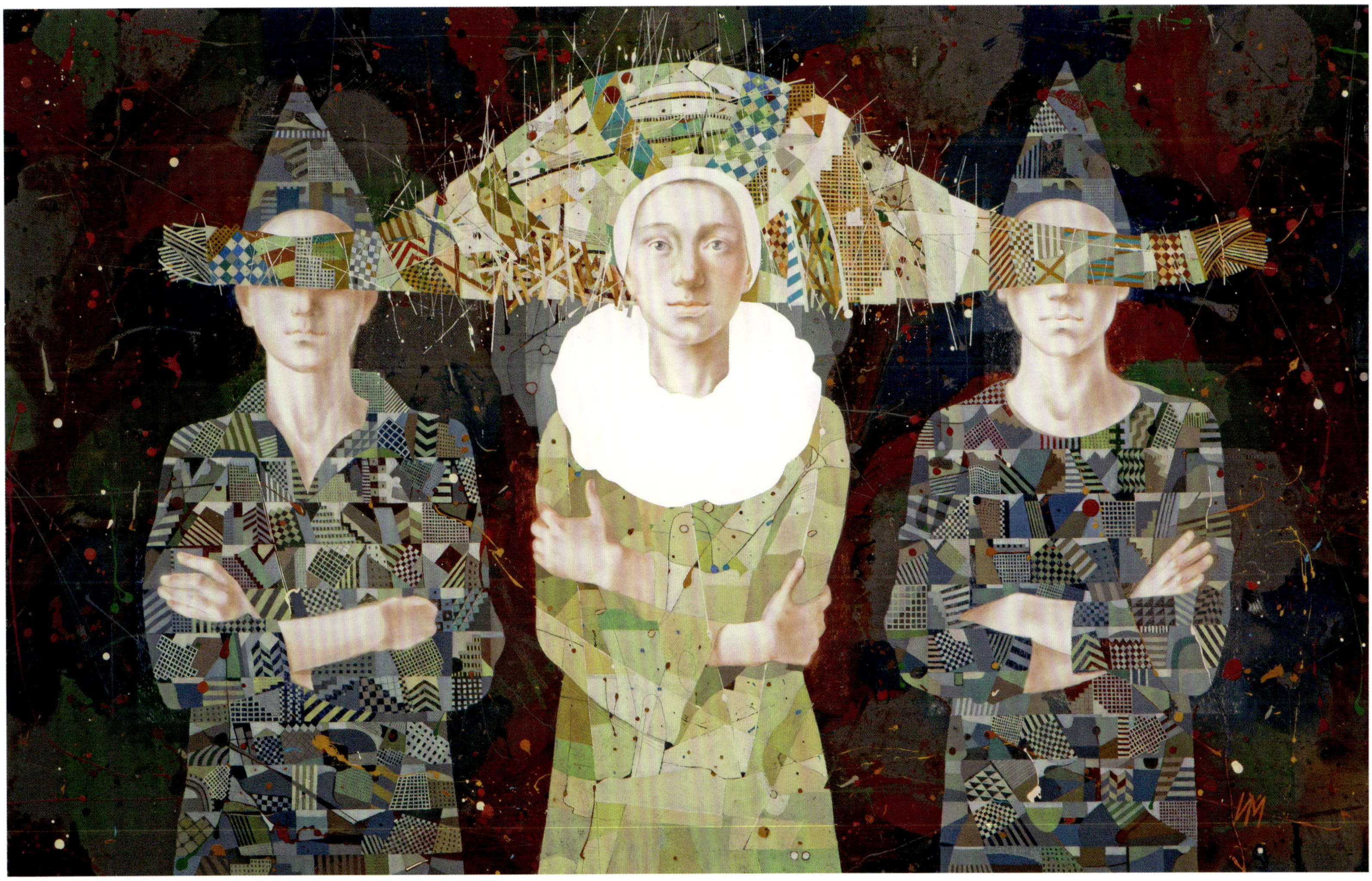

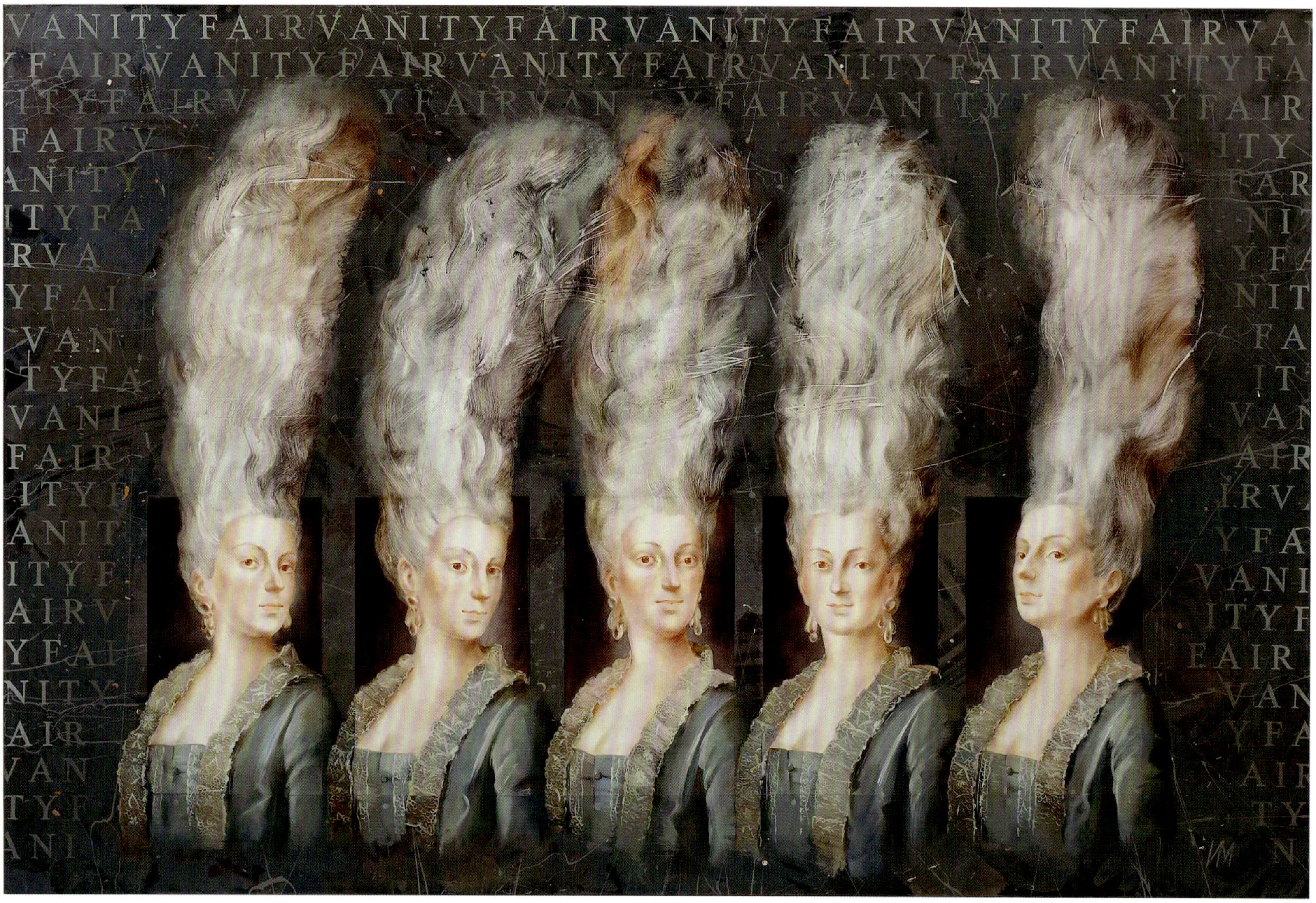

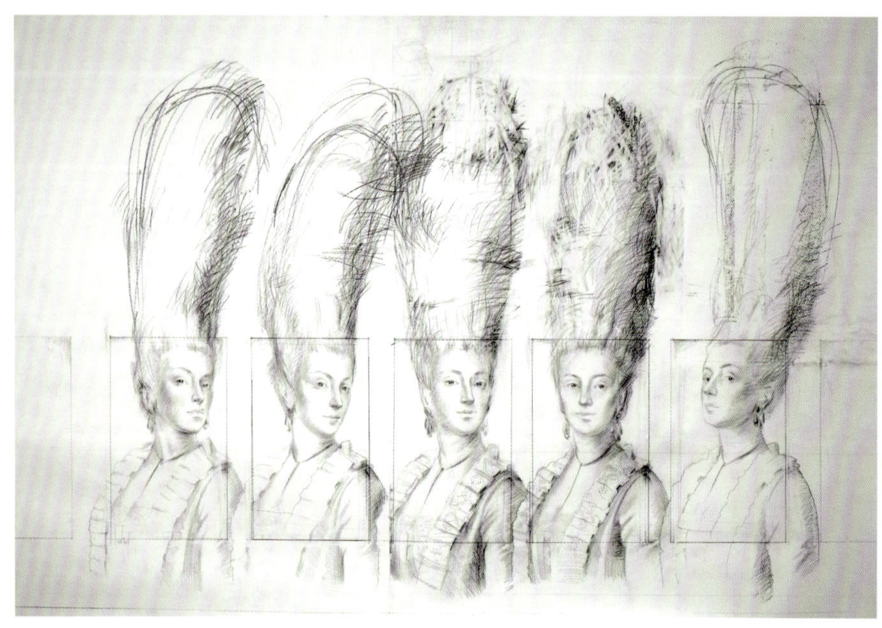

Vanity Fair, oil on canvas, 52 × 78"
(132 × 198 cm)

Vanity Fair, study, pencil on paper,
52 × 78" (132 × 198 cm)

Three Cornered Hat, oil on linen, 40 × 30"
(102 × 76 cm)

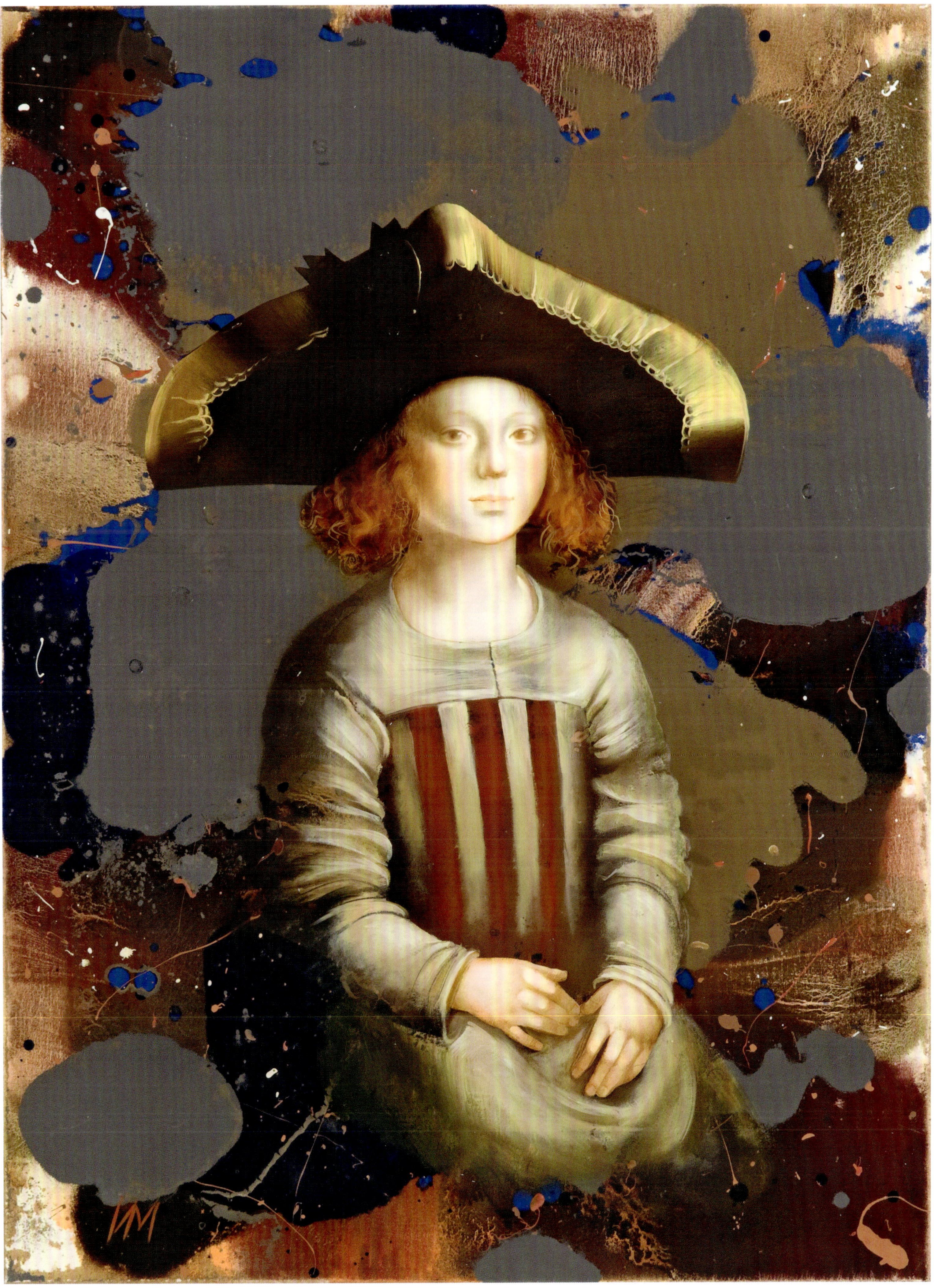

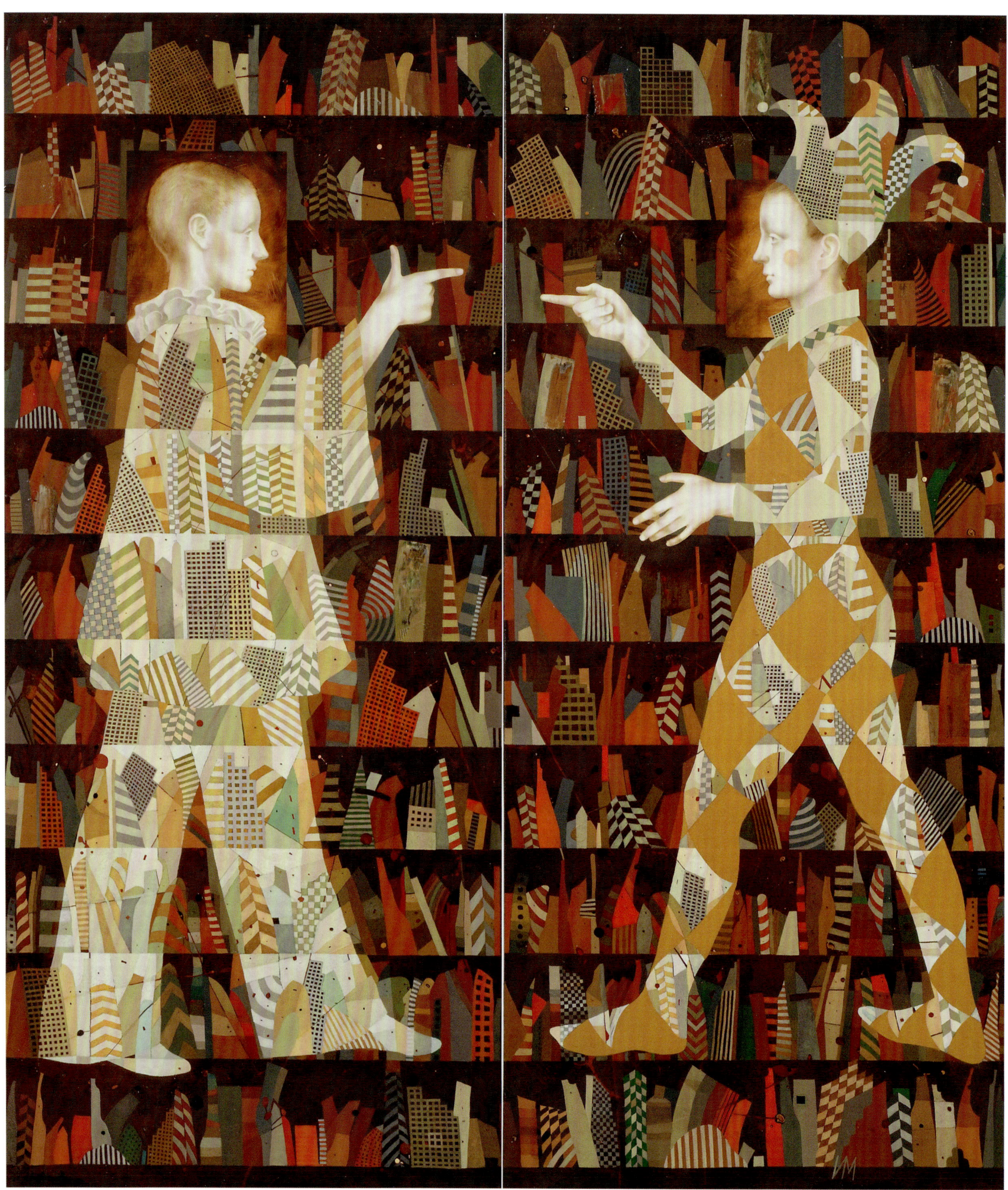

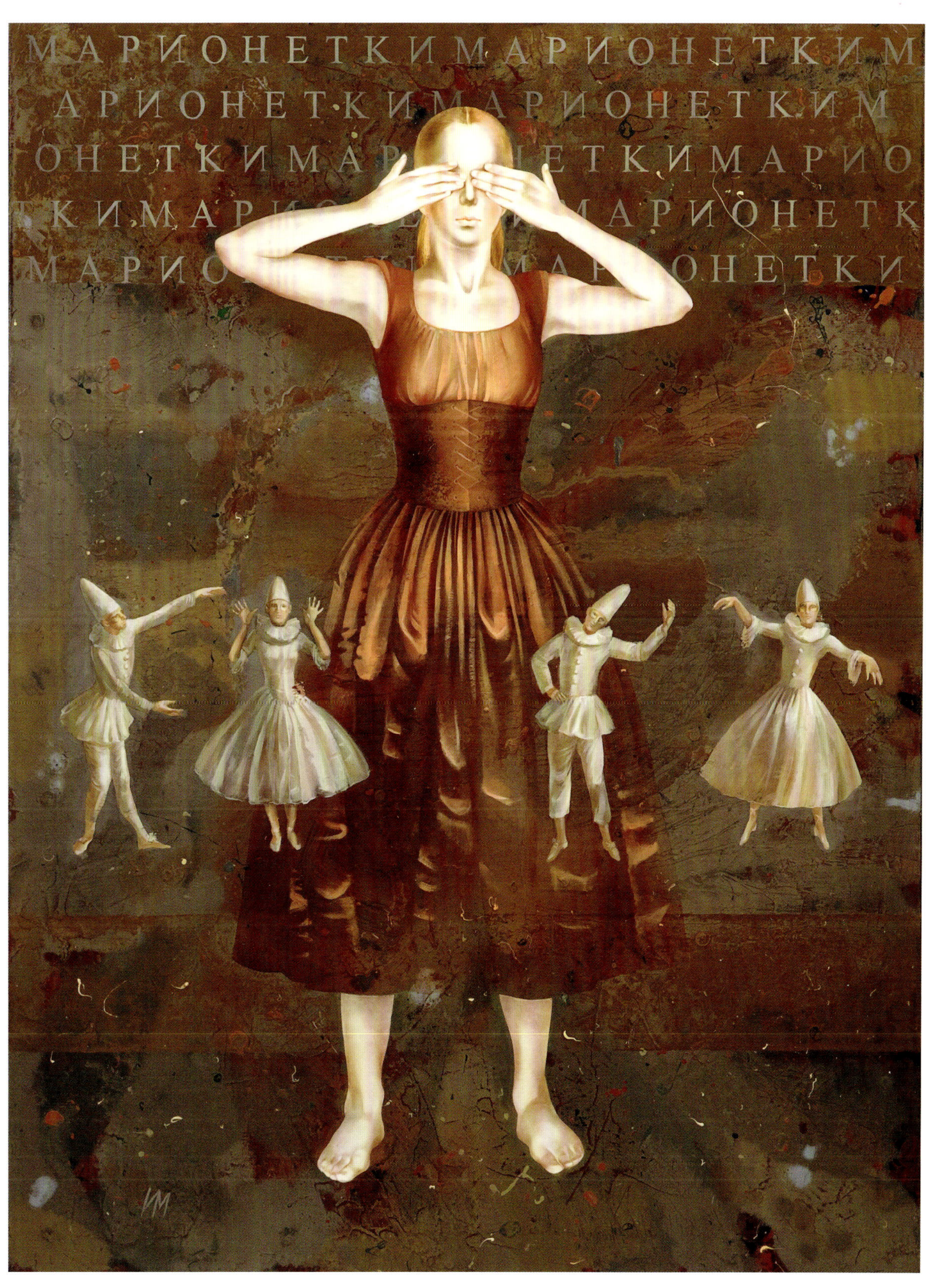

Pierrot & Harlequin (diptych), oil on canvas, 68 × 60″ (173 × 152 cm)

Marionettes, oil on canvas, 64 × 48″ (163 × 122 cm)

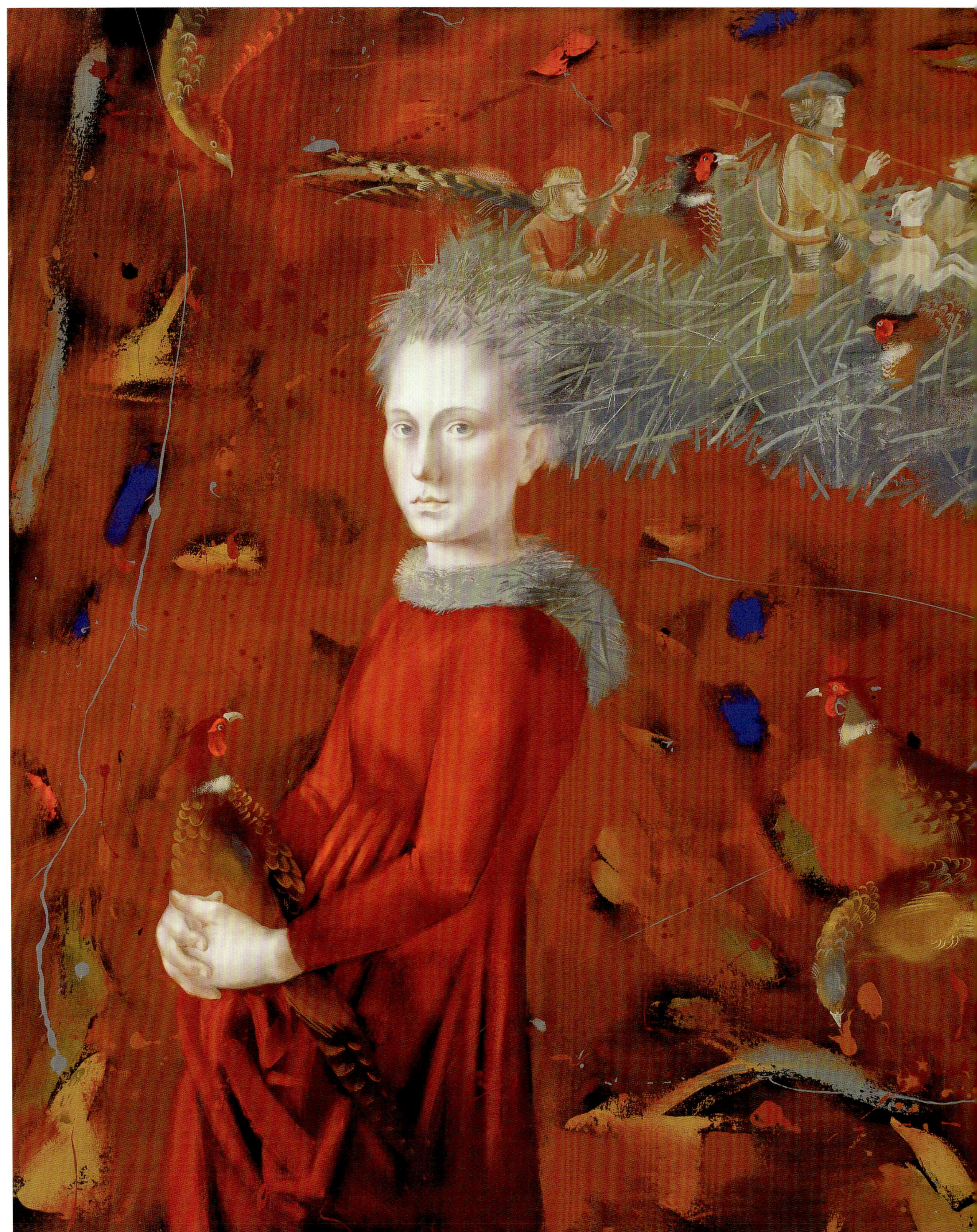

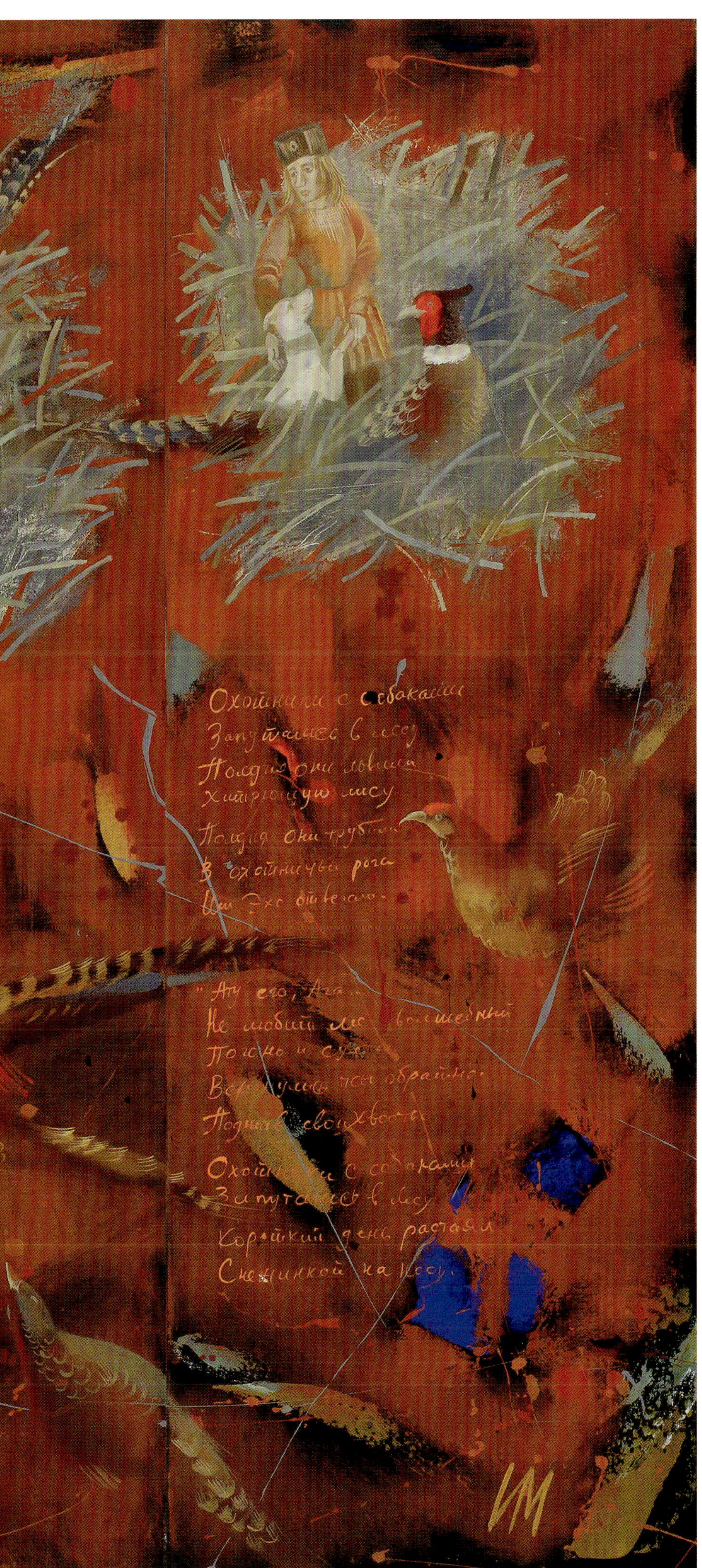

Where Pheasants Sleep (diptych),
oil on canvas, 40 × 52" (102 × 132 cm)

DÉJÀ VU SERIES

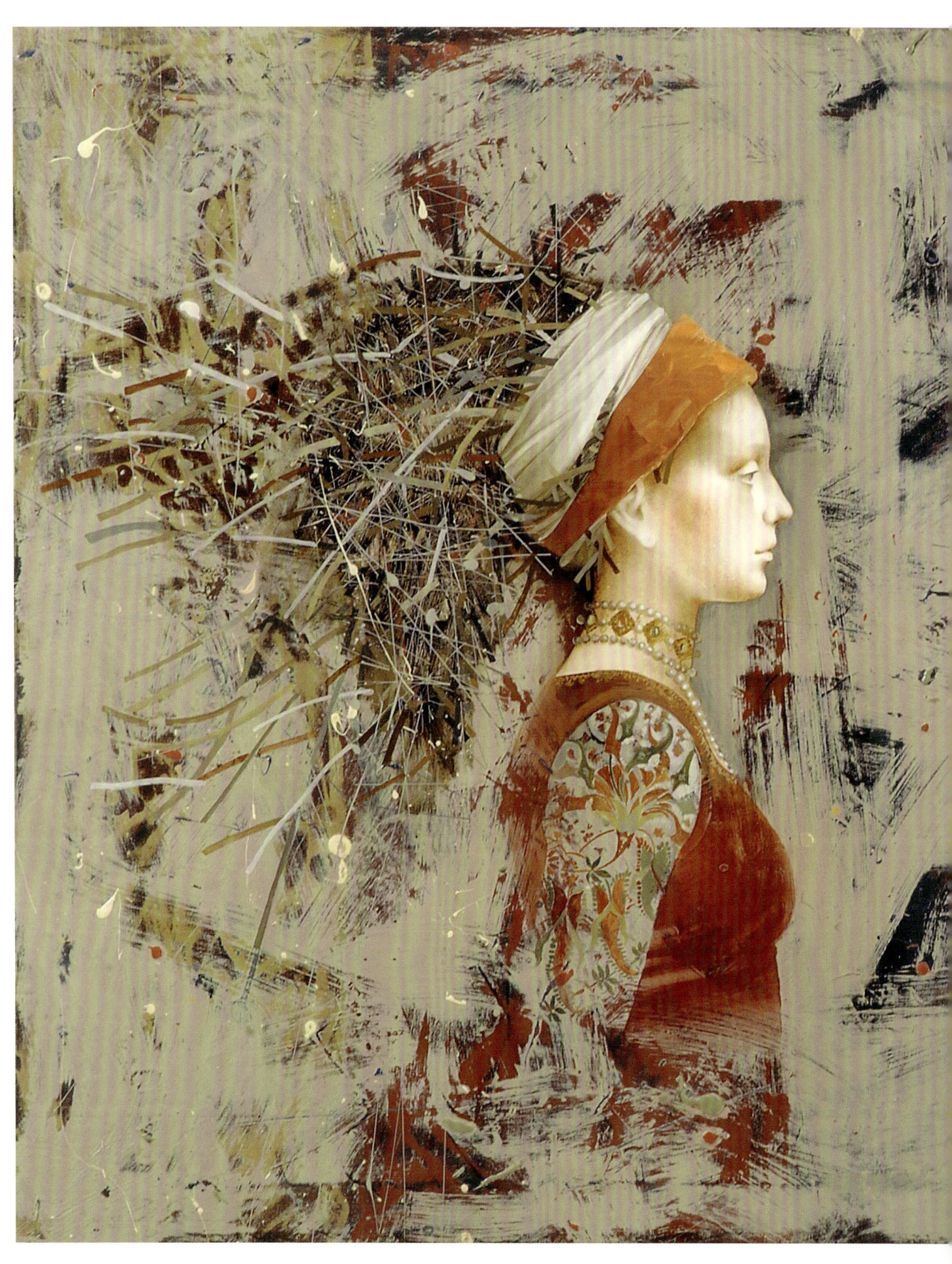

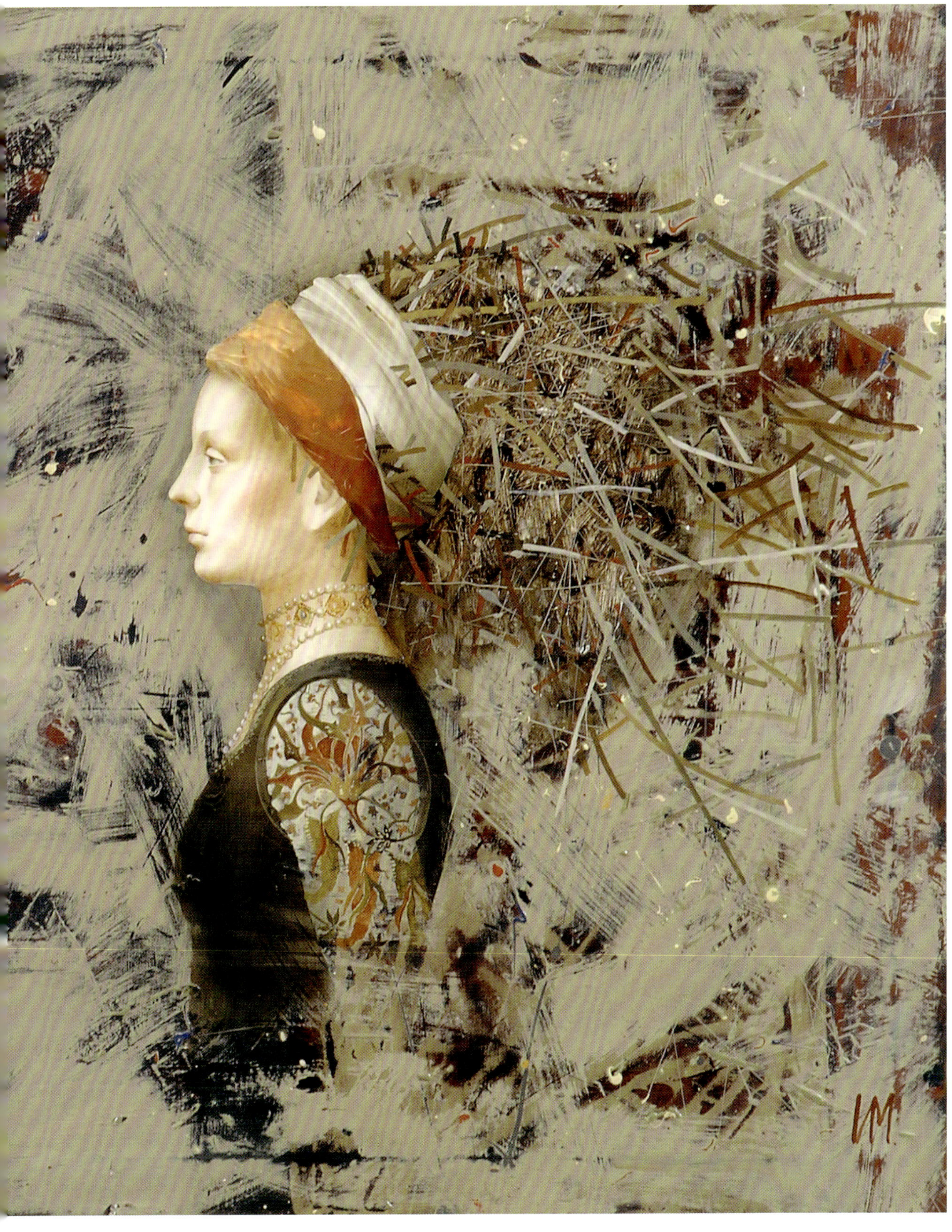

Cameo, oil on canvas, 32 × 52"
(81 × 132 cm)

Narcissus, oil on canvas, 60 × 60"
(152 × 152 cm)

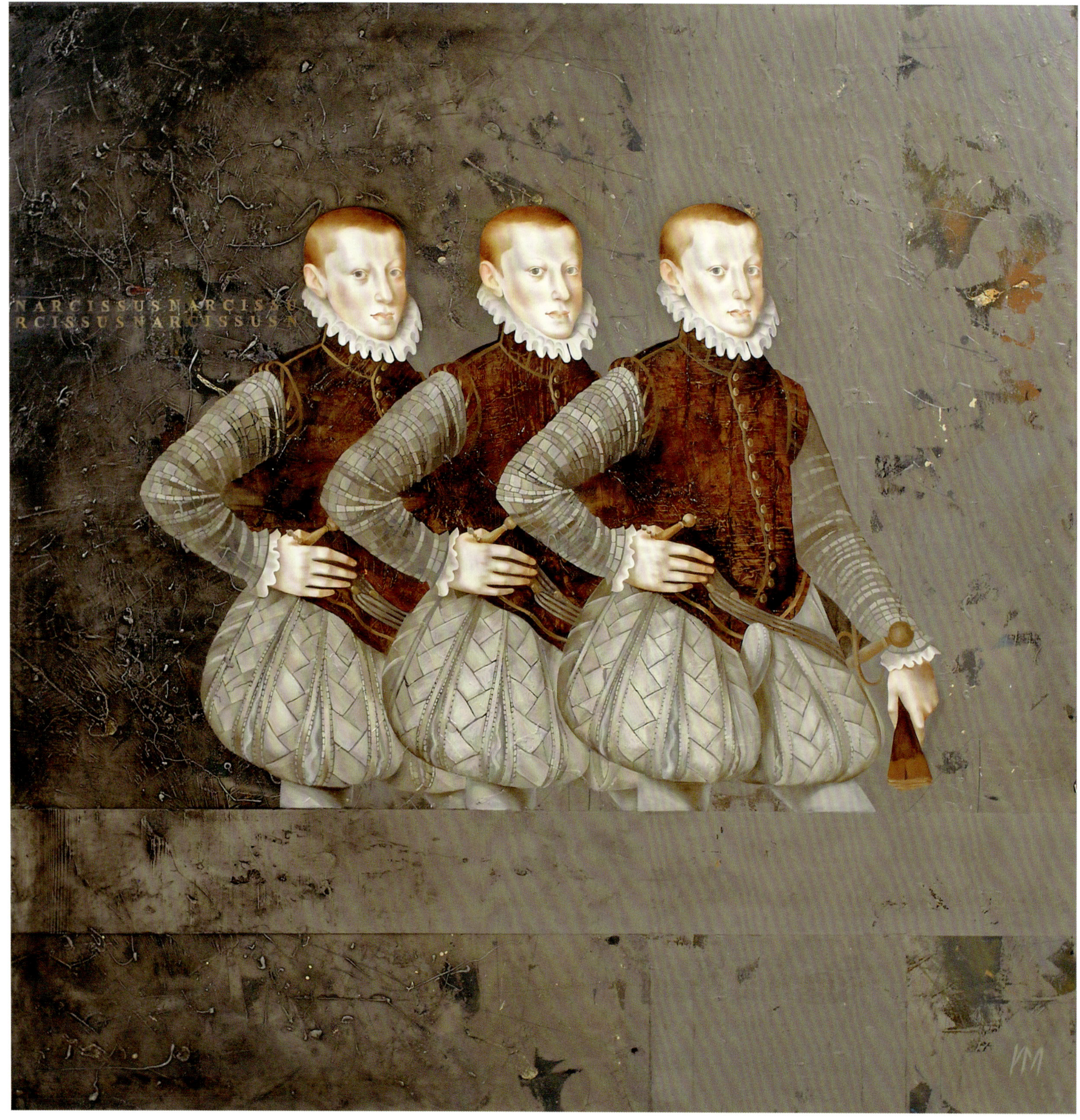

Behind the Looking Glass, oil on canvas,
48 × 66″ (122 × 168 cm)

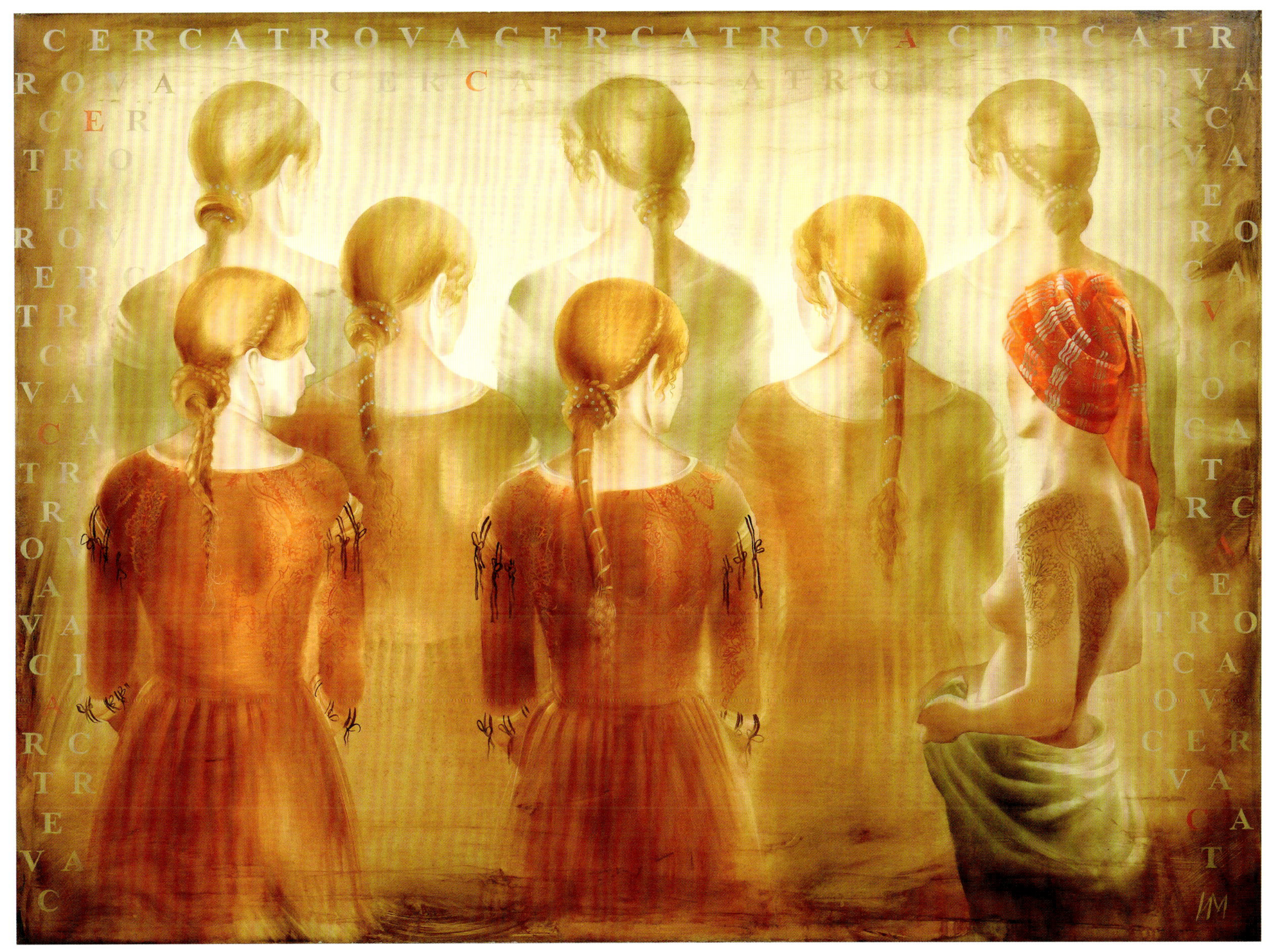

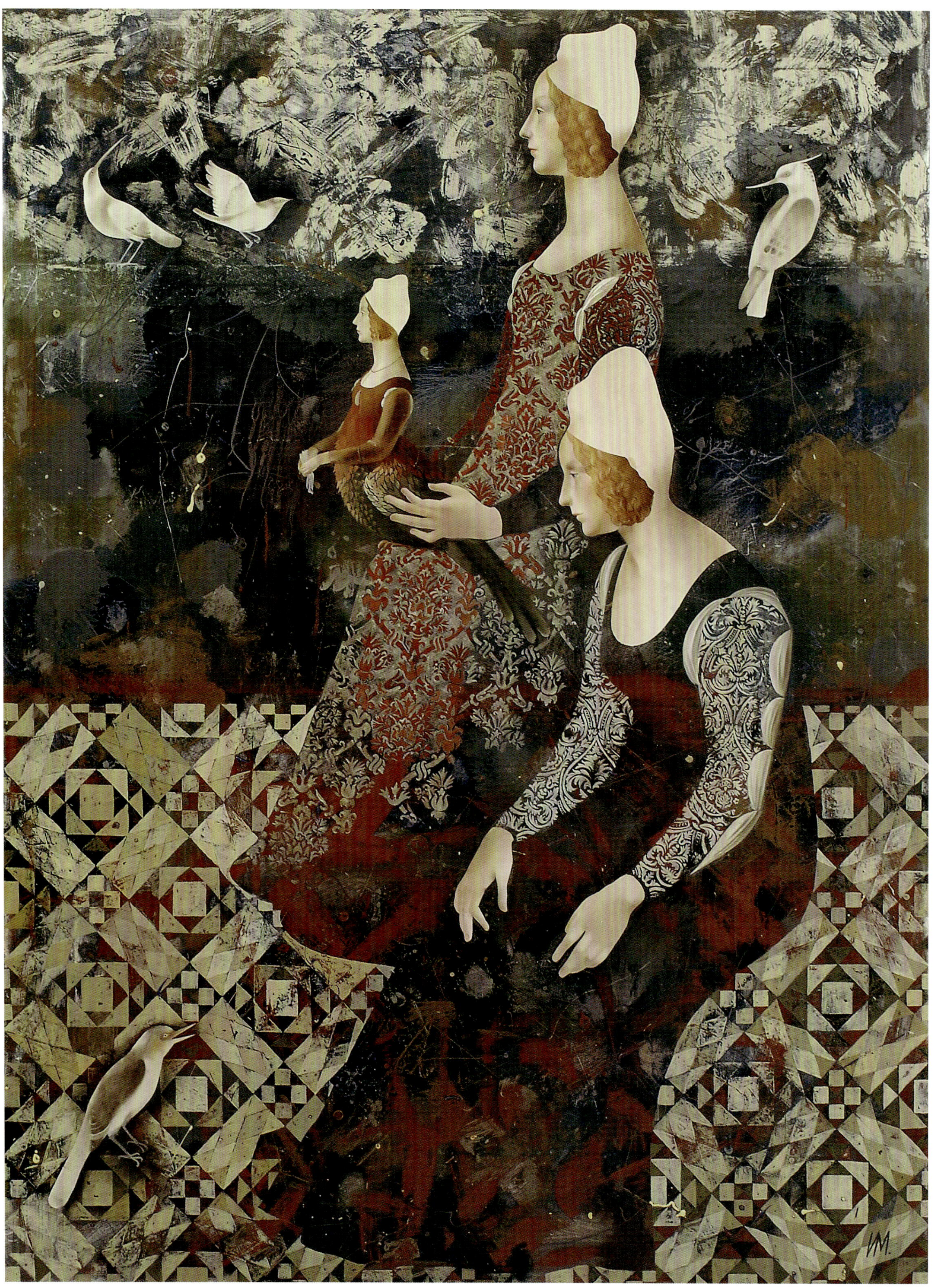

Les Oiseaux, oil on canvas, 64 × 48″
(163 × 122 cm)

Pomona, oil on canvas, 40 × 58″
(102 × 147 cm)

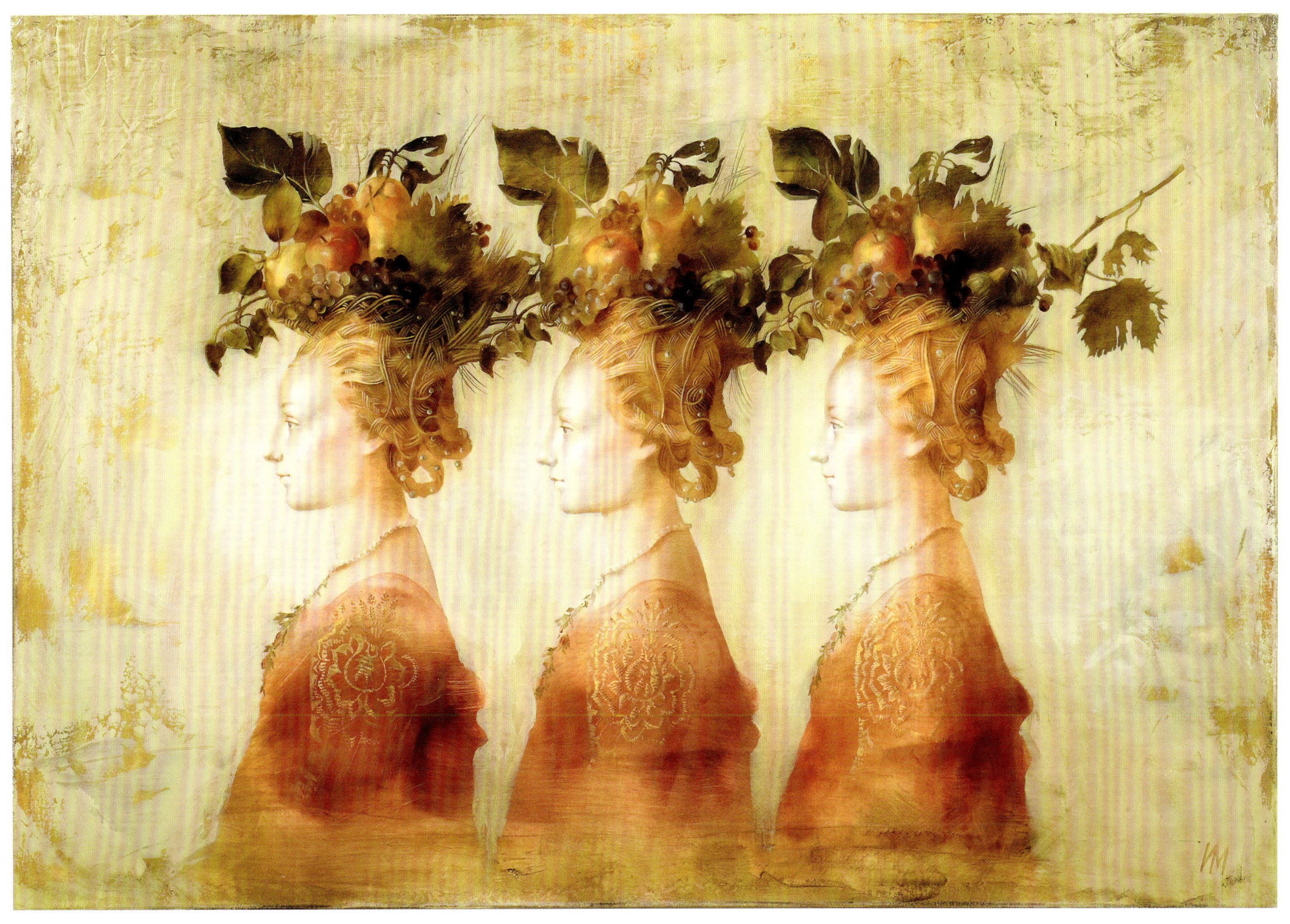

THE CATALOGUES SERIES

Shoes, Legs, What Else? (diptych),
oil on canvas, 70 × 64" (178 × 163 cm)

Quelle Heure Est-il, oil on canvas, 60 × 48"
(153 × 122 cm)

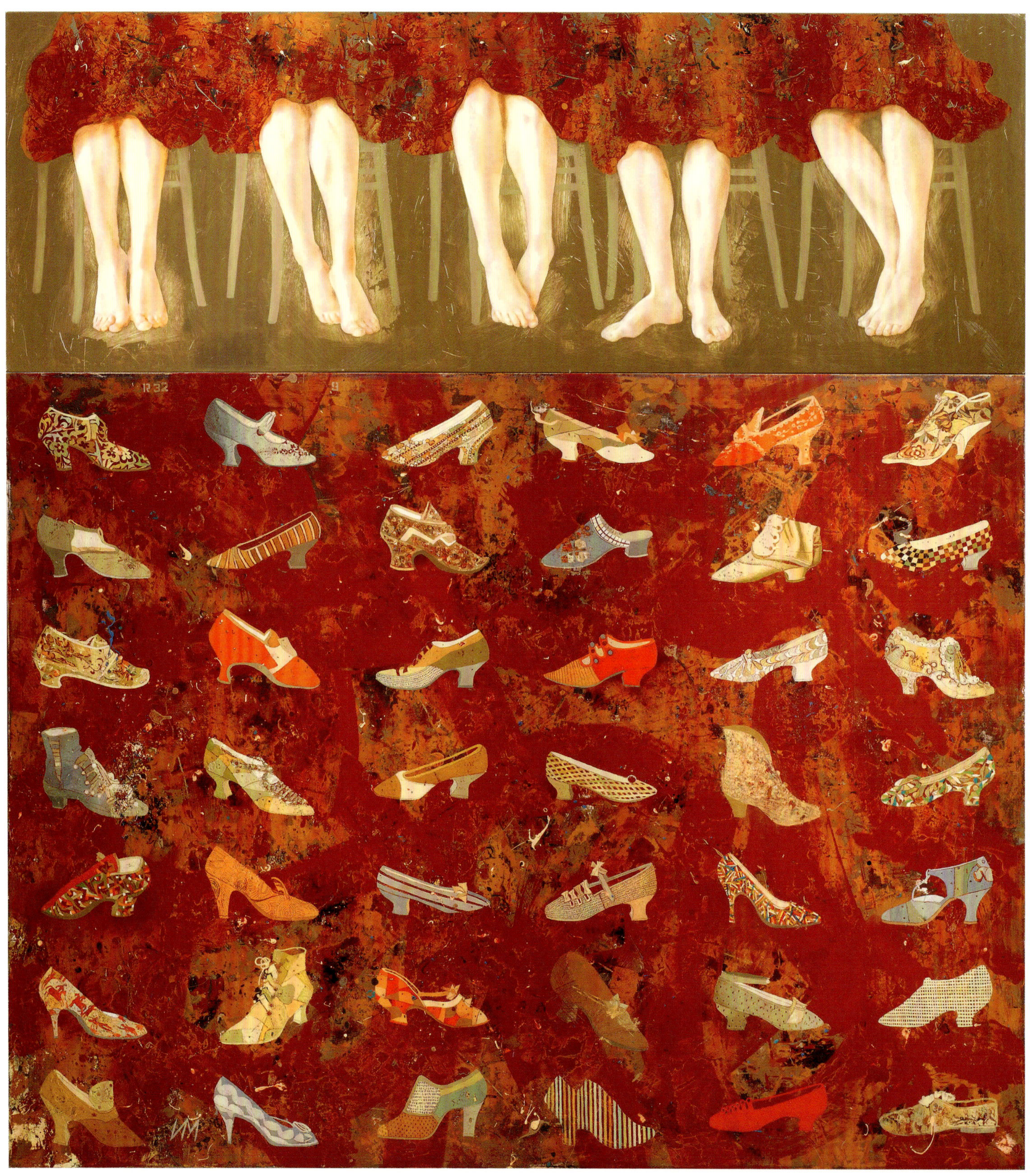

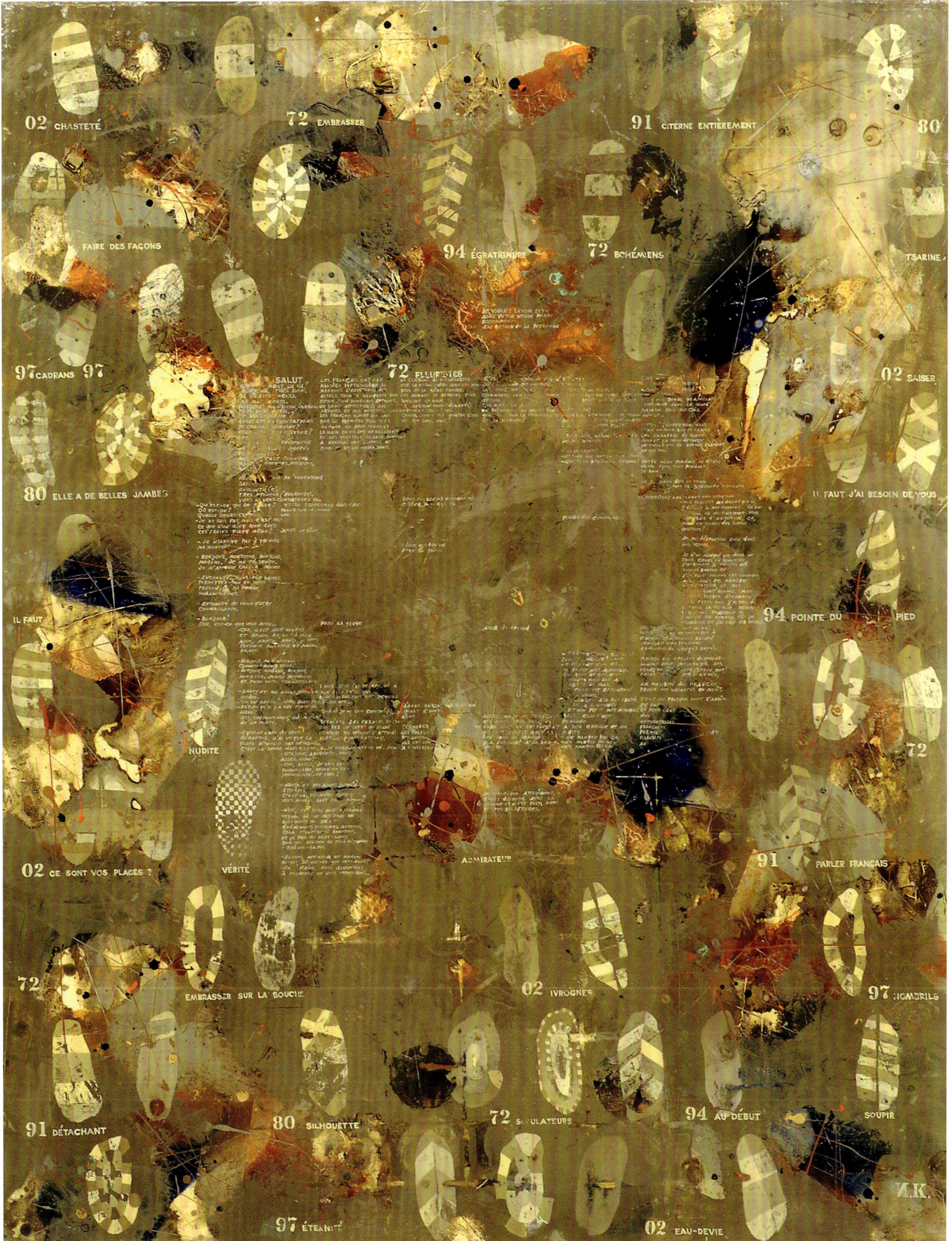

02 CHASTETÉ
72 EMBRASSER
91 CITERNE ENTIÈREMENT
80
FAIRE DES FAÇONS
94 ÉGRATIGNURE
72 BOHÉMIENS
TSARINE
97 CADRANS 97
SALUT
72 FLEURISTES
02 BAISER
80 ELLE A DE BELLES JAMBES
IL FAUT J'AI BESOIN DE VOUS
IL FAUT
94 POINTE DU PIED
NUDITÉ
72
02 CE SONT VOS PLACES ?
VÉRITÉ
ADMIRATEUR
91 PARLER FRANÇAIS
72
EMBRASSER SUR LA BOUCHE
02 IVROGNES
97 NOMBRILS
91 DÉTACHANT
80 SILHOUETTE
72 SPÉCULATEURS
94 AU DÉBUT
SOUPIR
97 ÉTERNEL
02 EAU-DE-VIE
I.K.

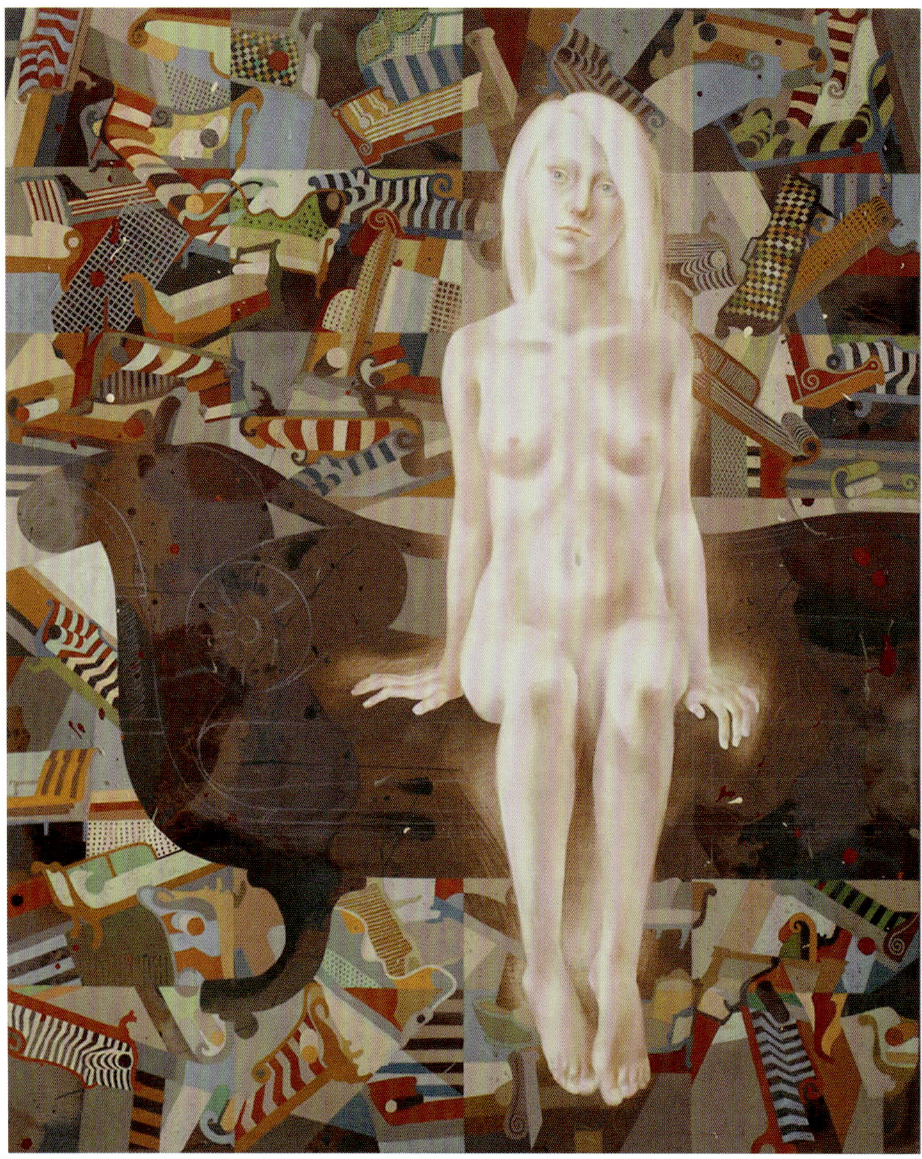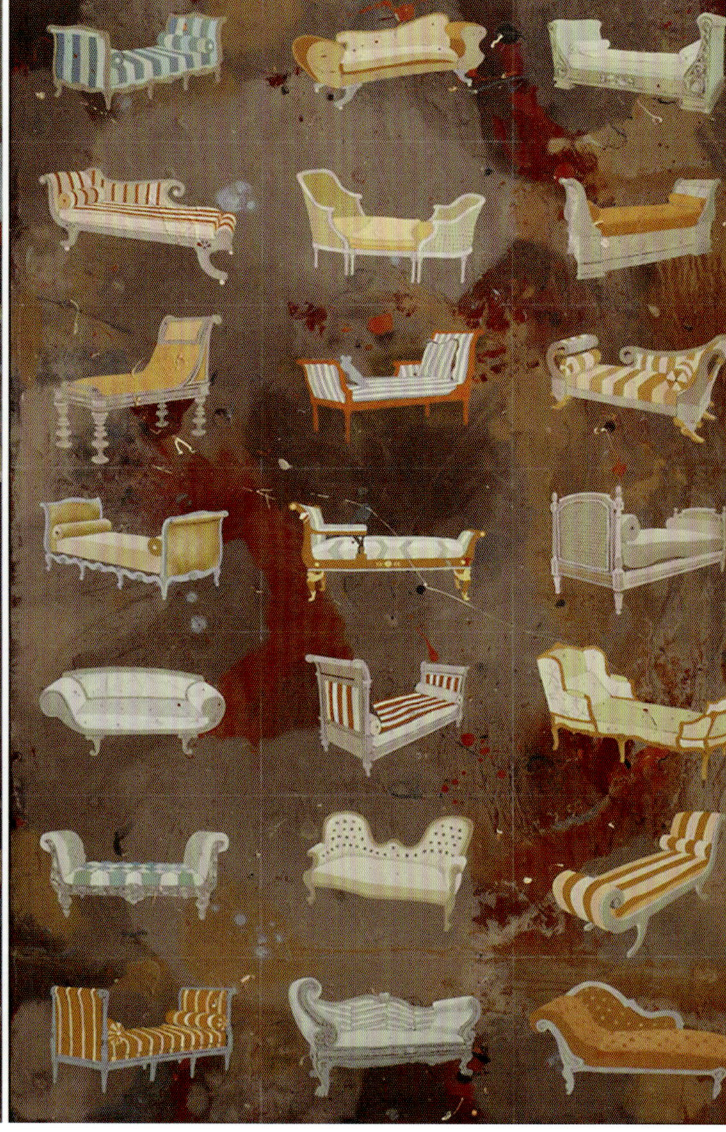

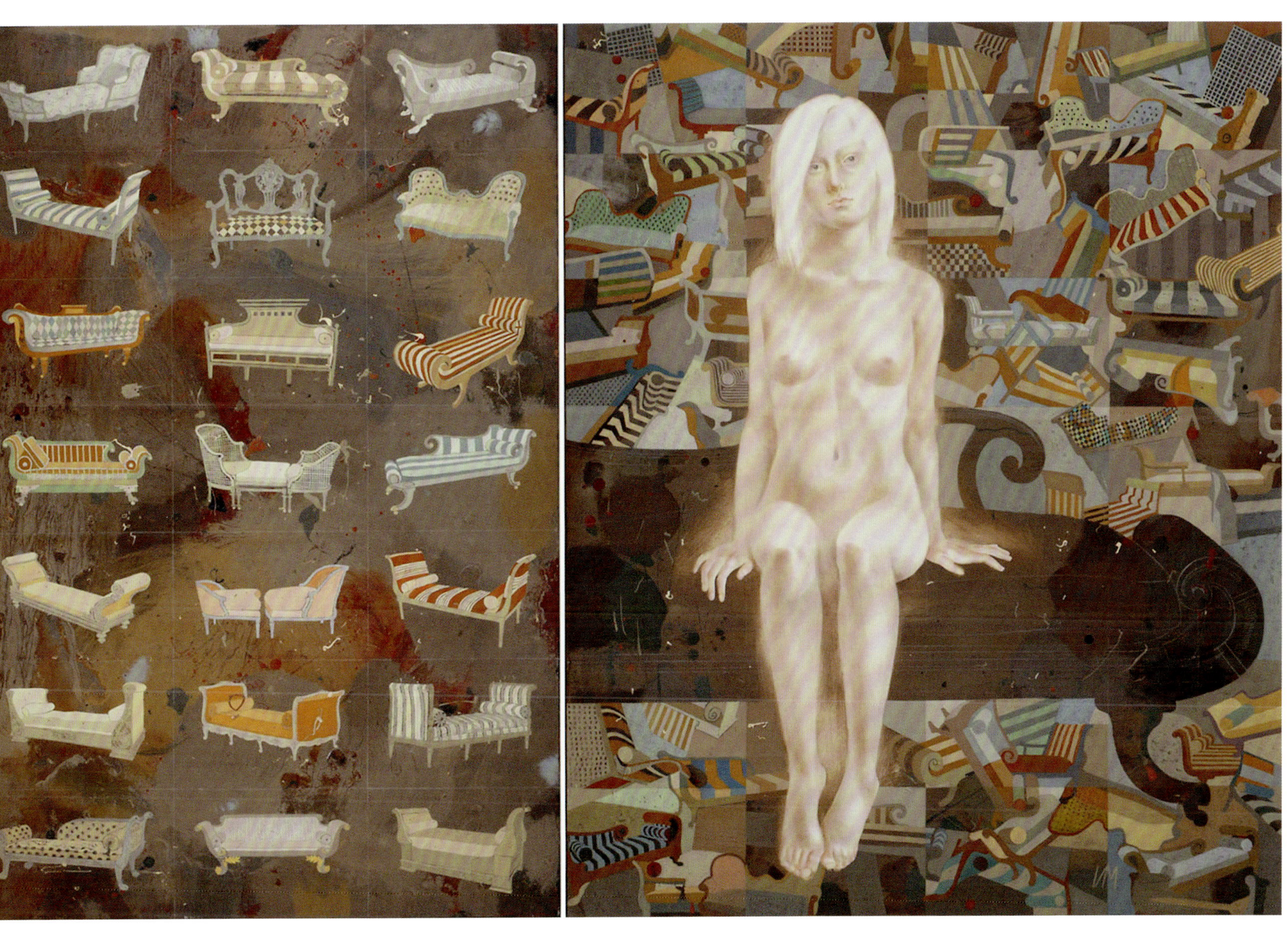

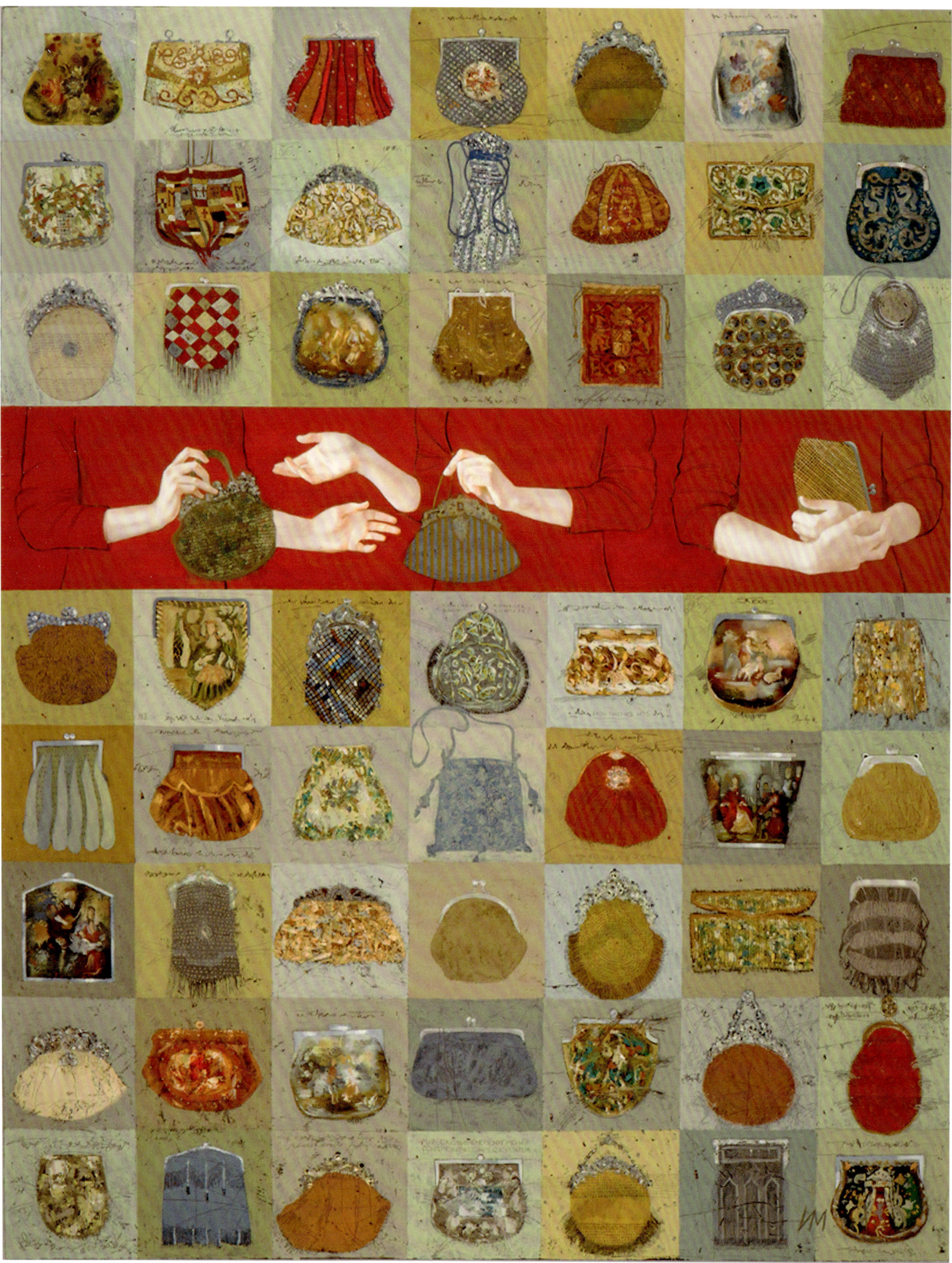

Hold Tight & Carry On, oil on canvas,
64 × 50" (163 × 127 cm)

Viene La Sera, oil on canvas, 61 × 48"
(155 × 122 cm)

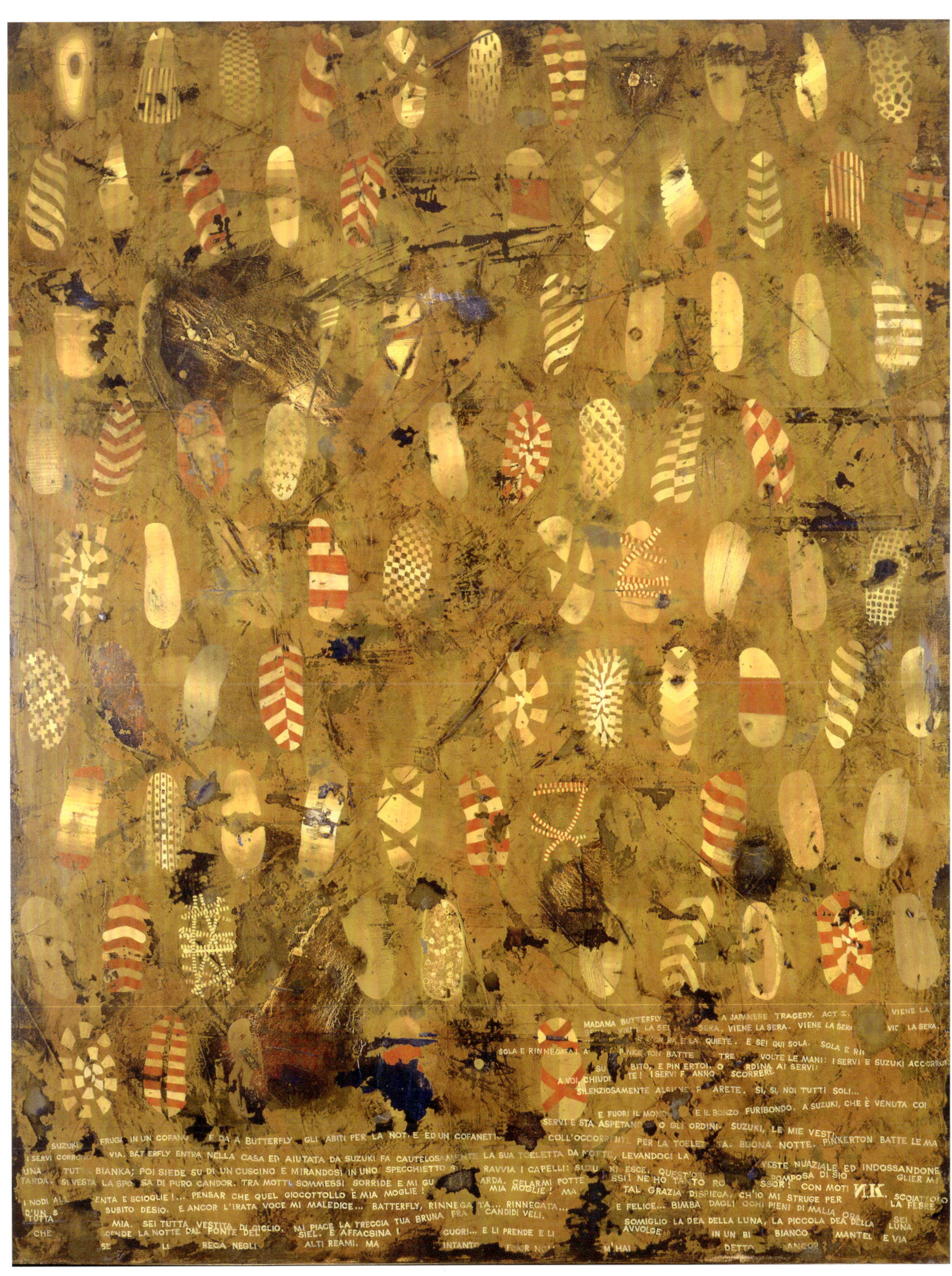

THE WALKERS PROJECT SERIES

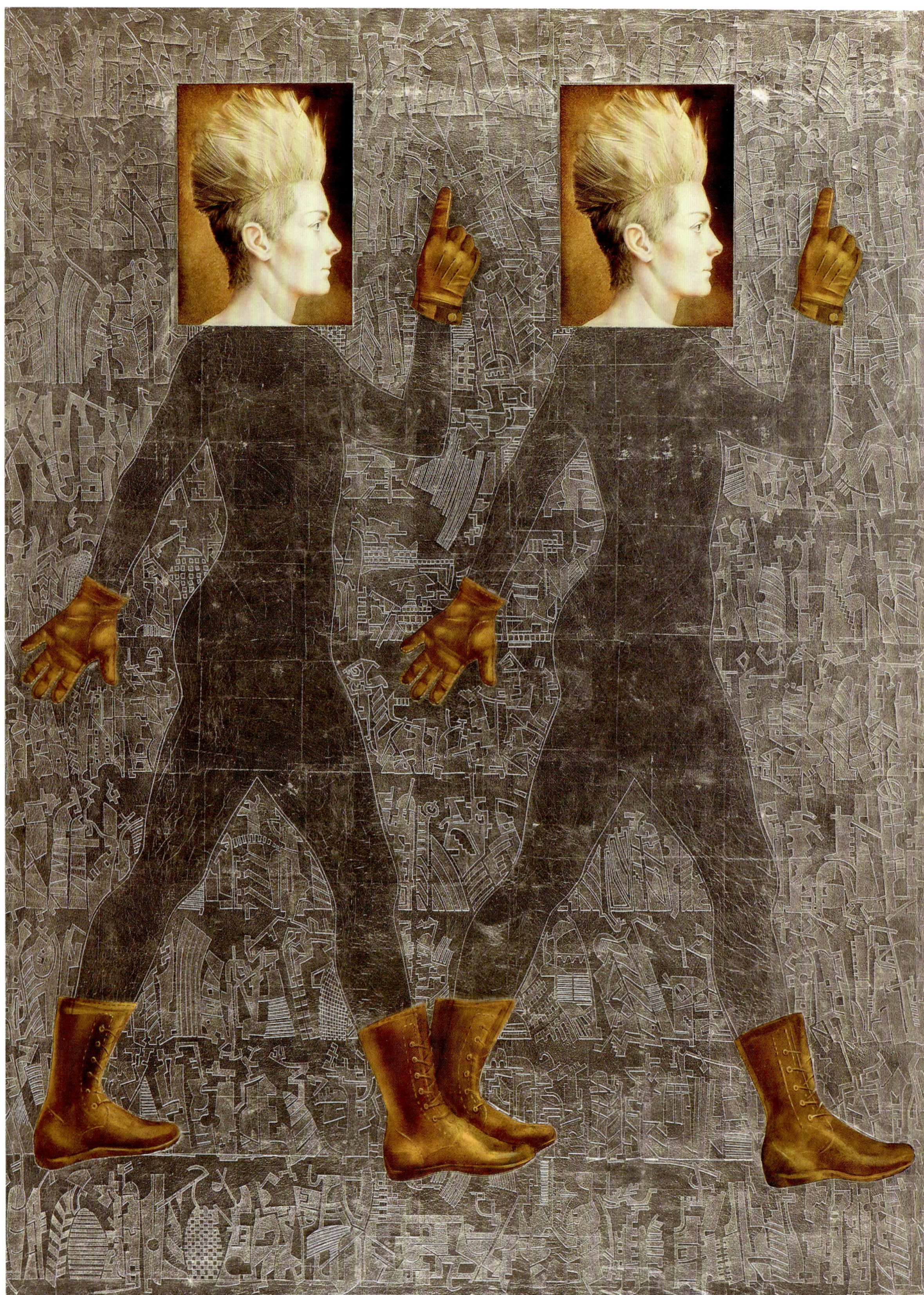

Walkers-XVIII (Time Travelers), oil, acrylic, 12K white gold leaf on canvas, 64 × 48" (163 × 122 cm)

Painting for the Sky (diptych), oil on canvas, 83 × 58" (211 × 147 cm)

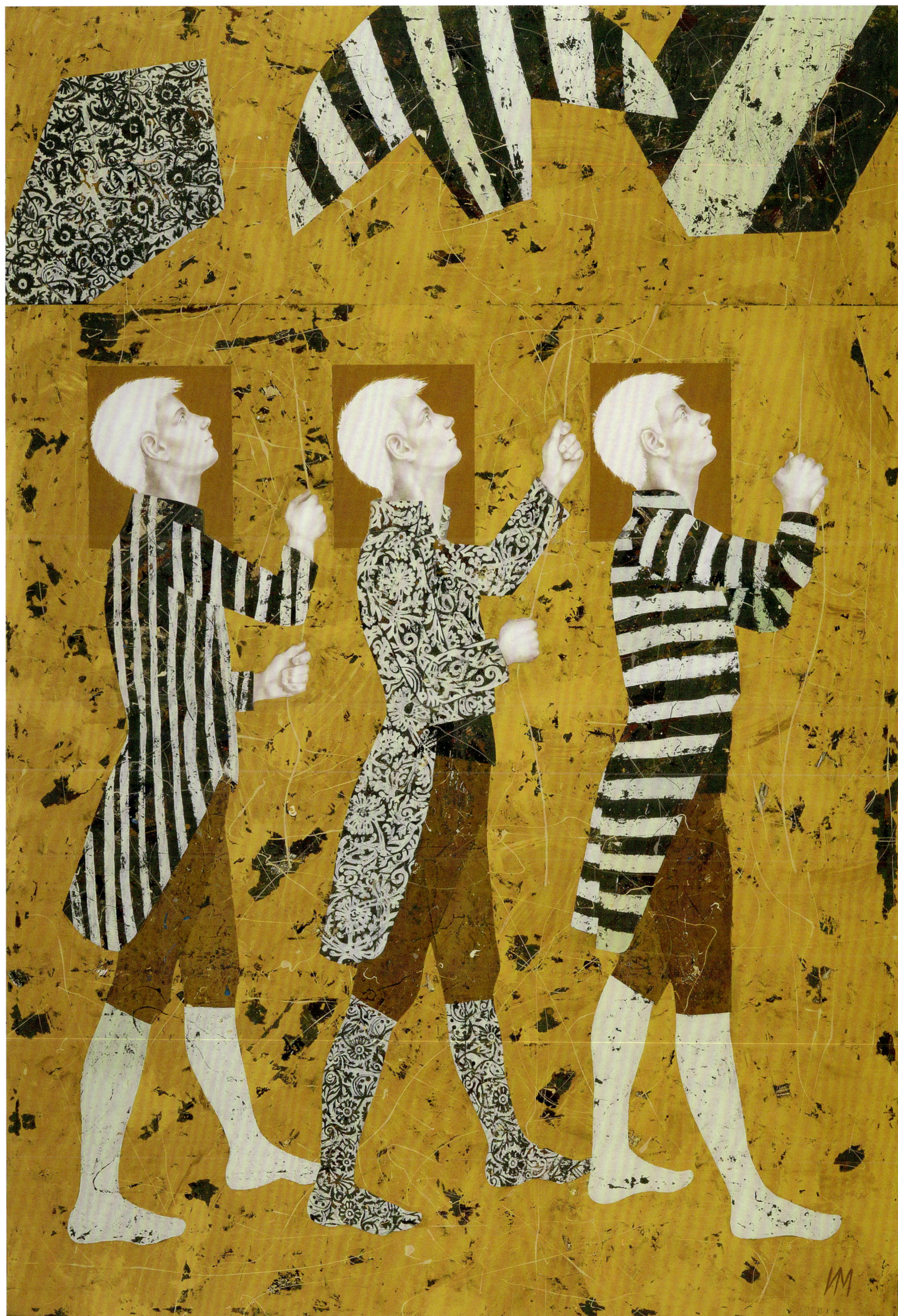

SILVER ILLUSIONS SERIES

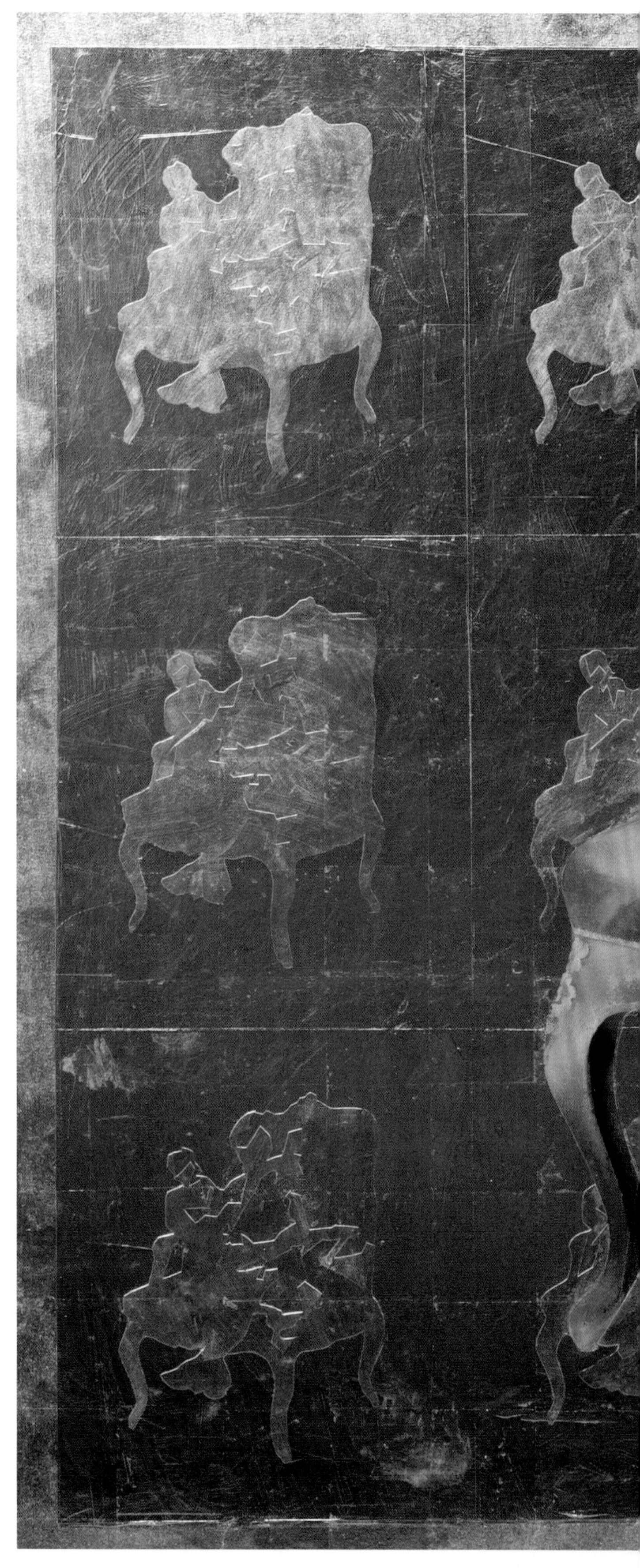

Un Fauteuil Ancien, oil on canvas,
12K white gold leaf (3D), 45 × 63″
(114 × 160 cm)

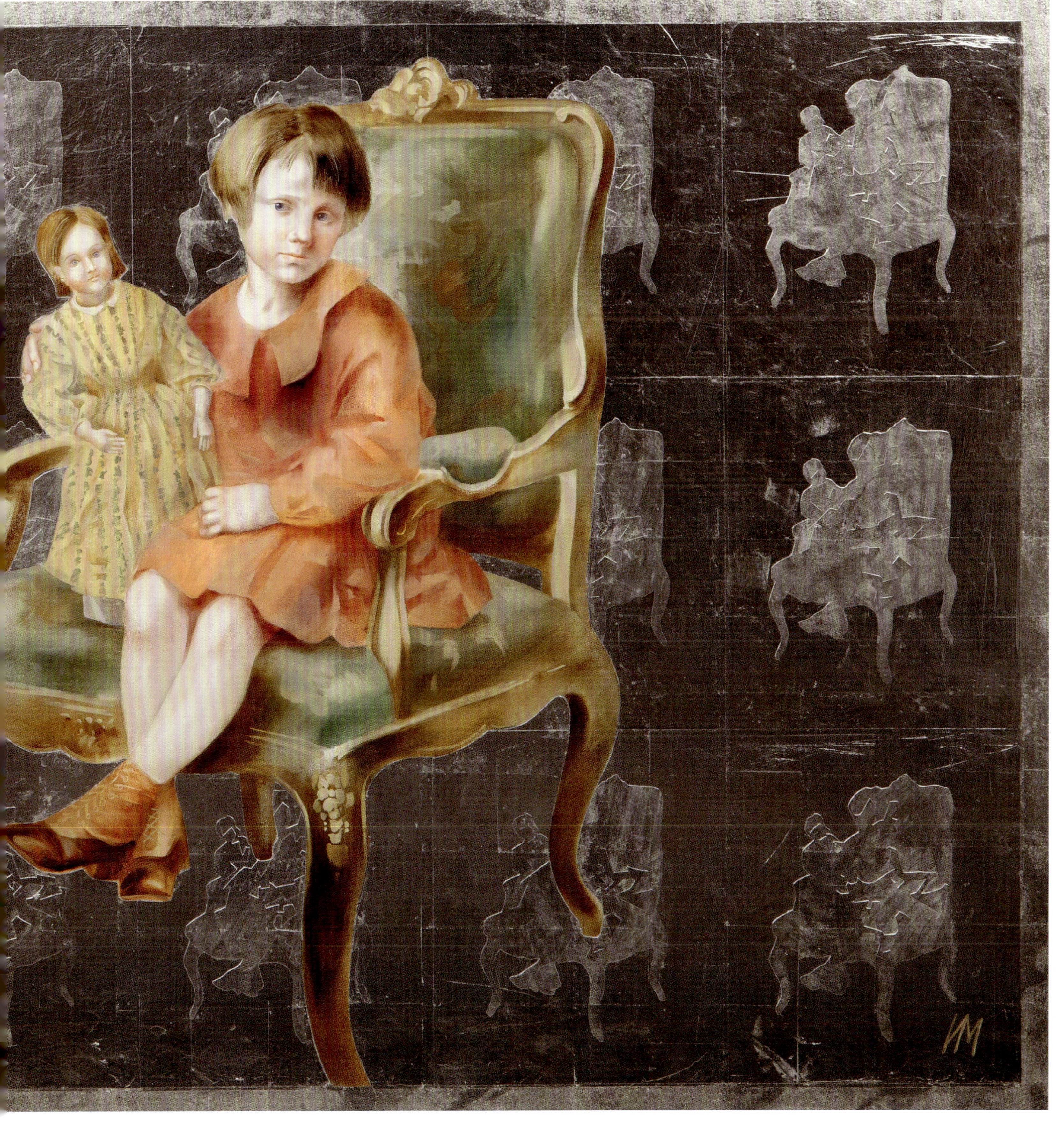

SILK ROAD SERIES

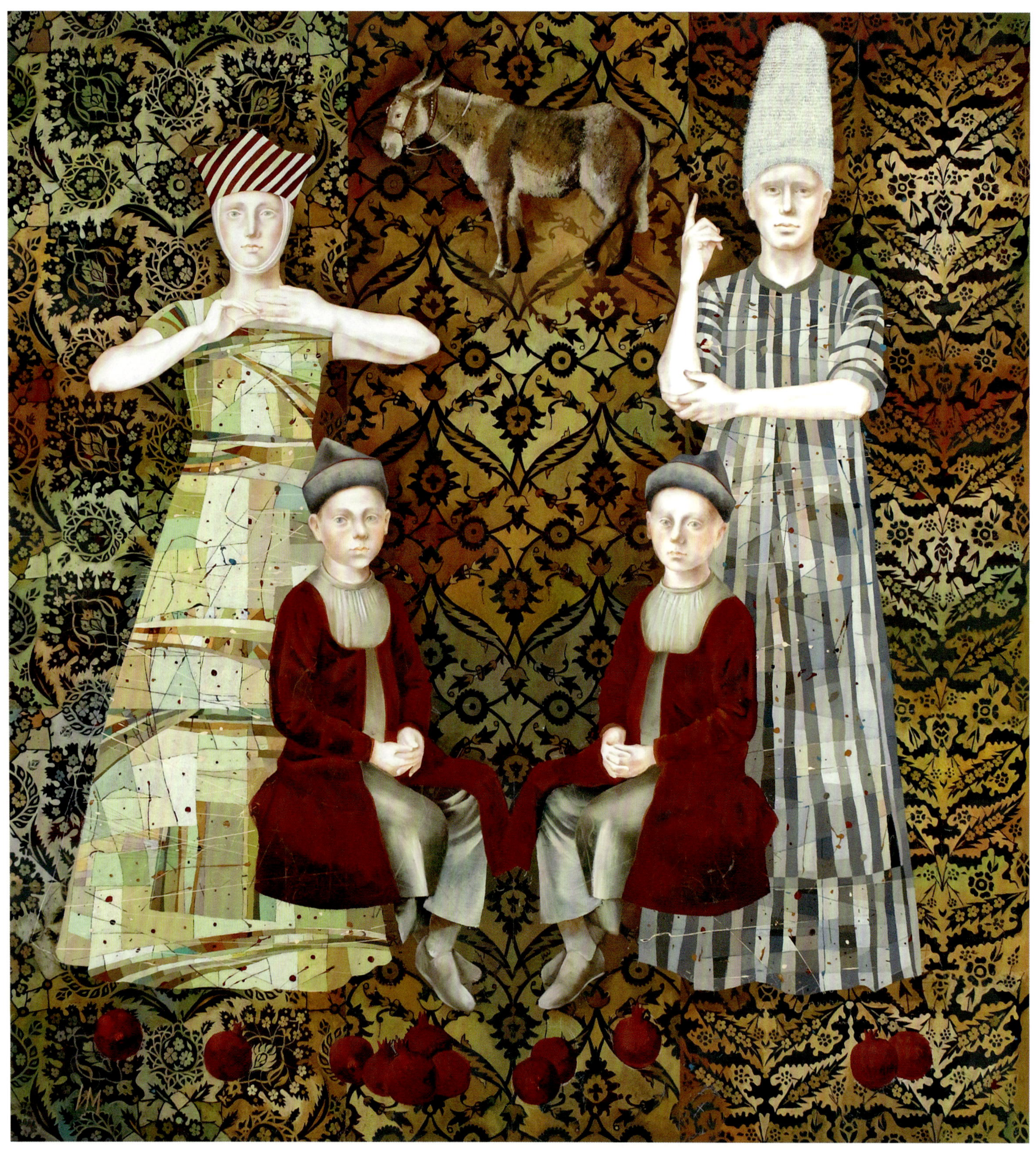

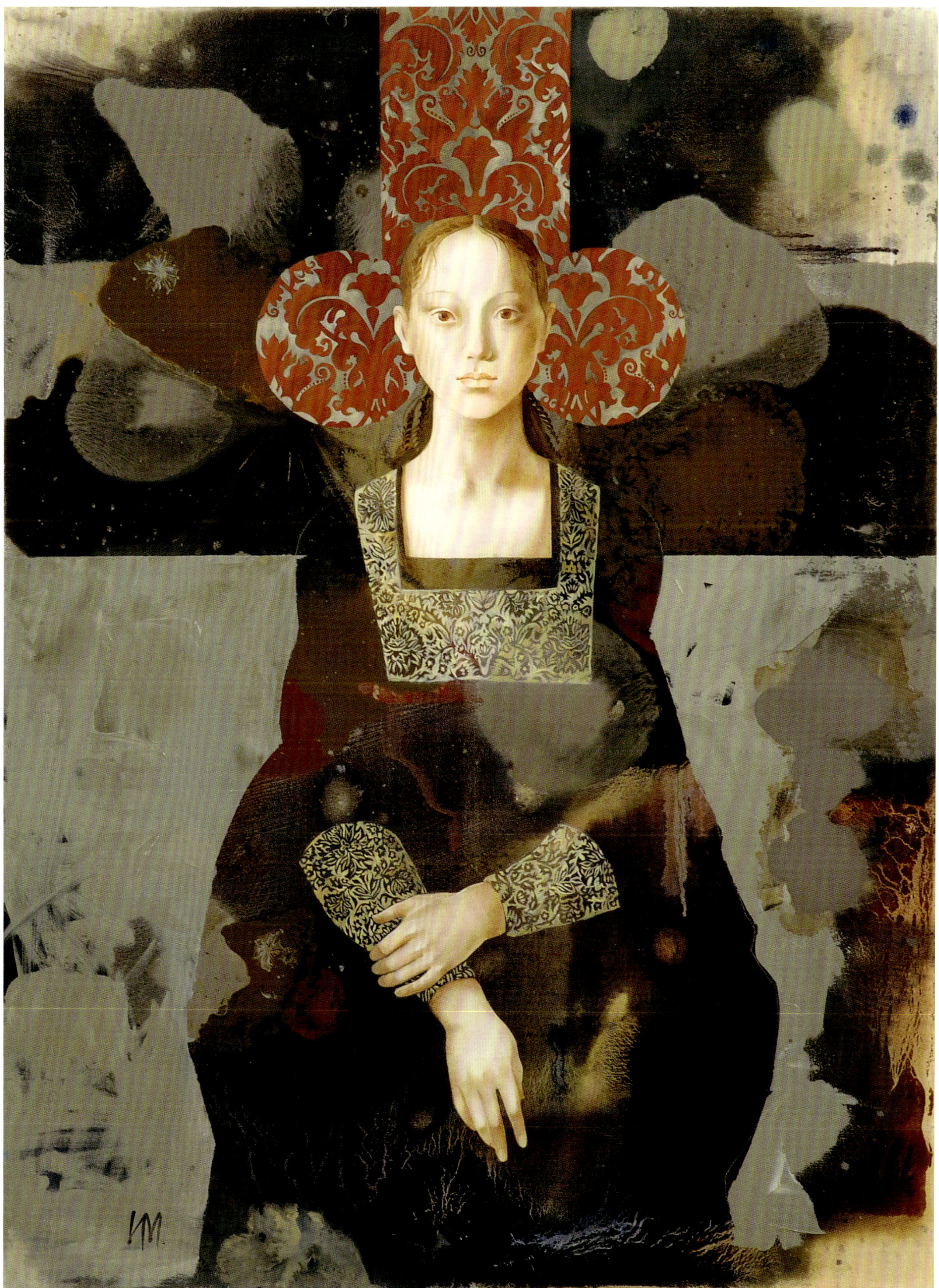

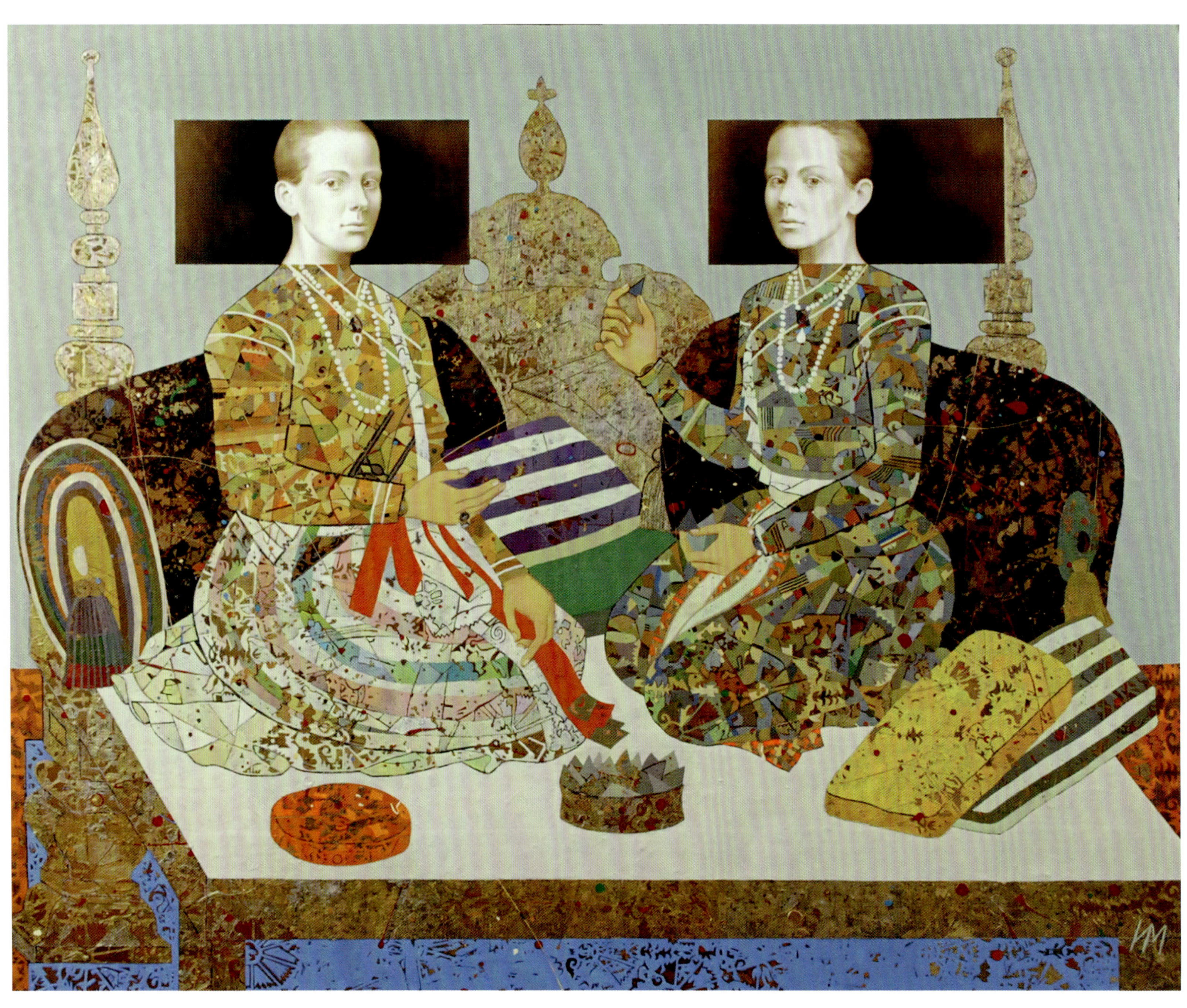

Tea with Maharaja, oil on canvas, 46 × 58″
(117 × 147 cm)

Painted Fans (diptych), oil on canvas,
42 × 64" (107 × 163 cm)

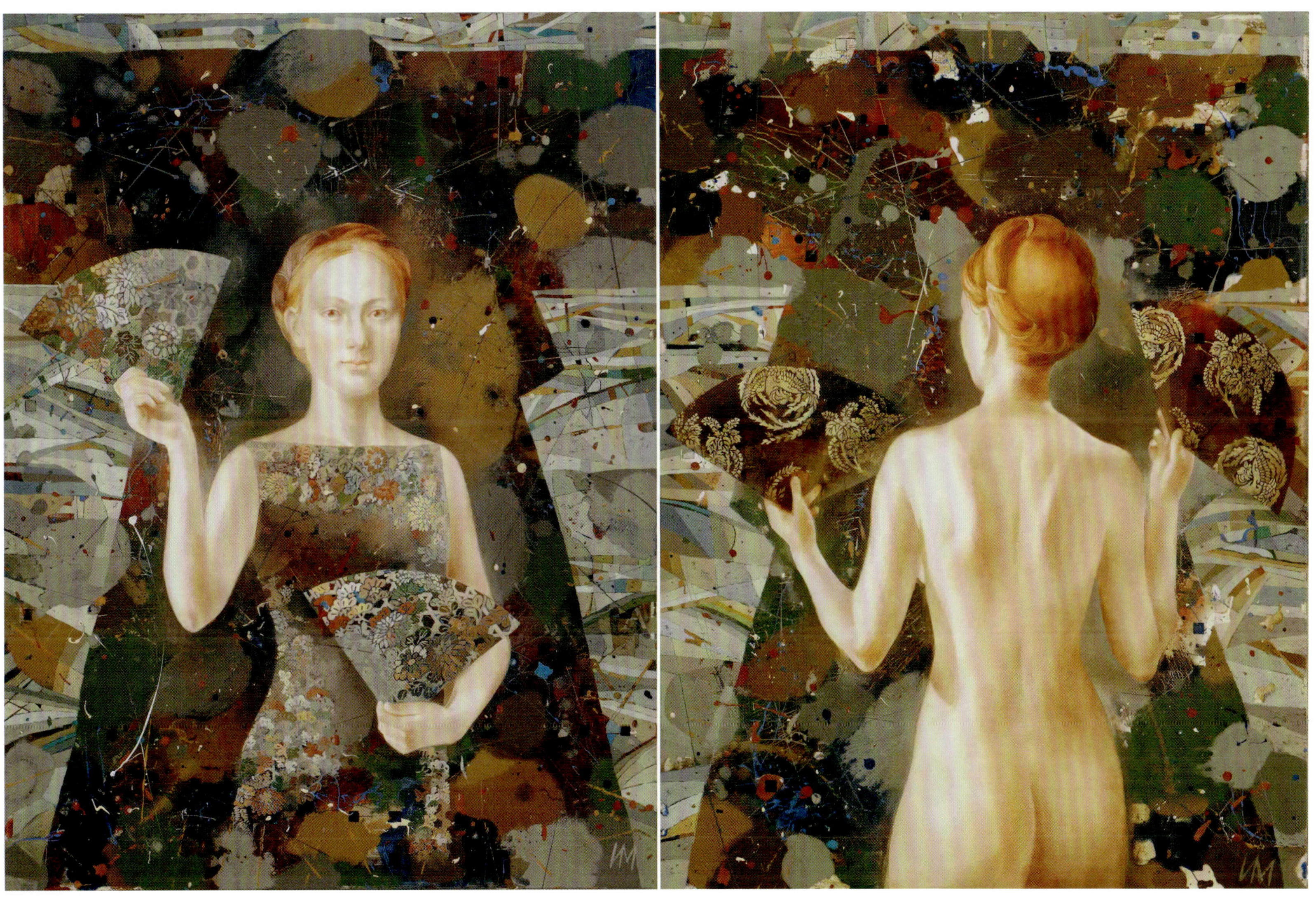

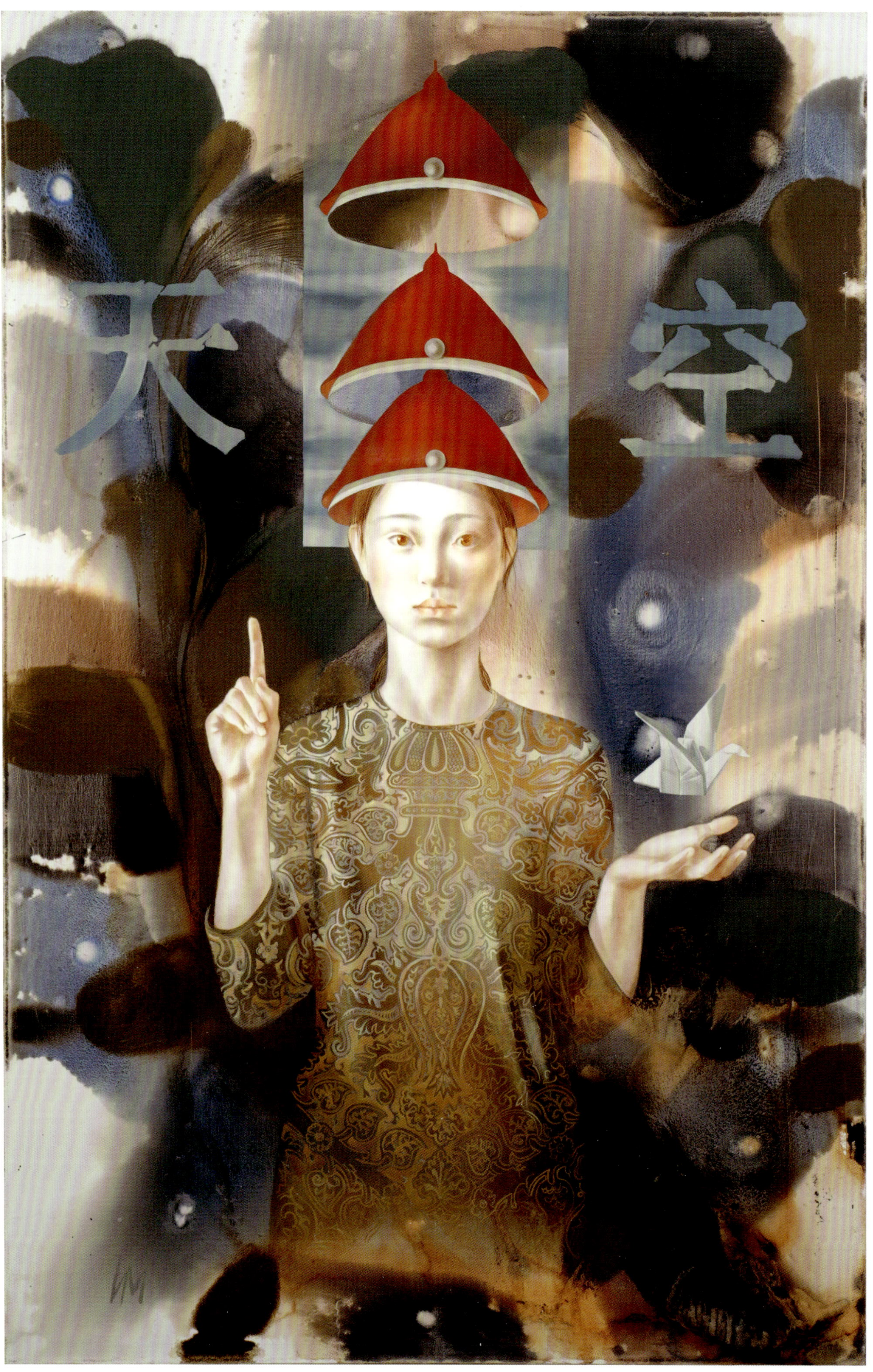

天
空

Sky, oil on canvas, 58 × 38″ (147 × 97 cm)

Guardians of the Sound, oil on canvas,
42 × 65″ (107 × 165 cm)

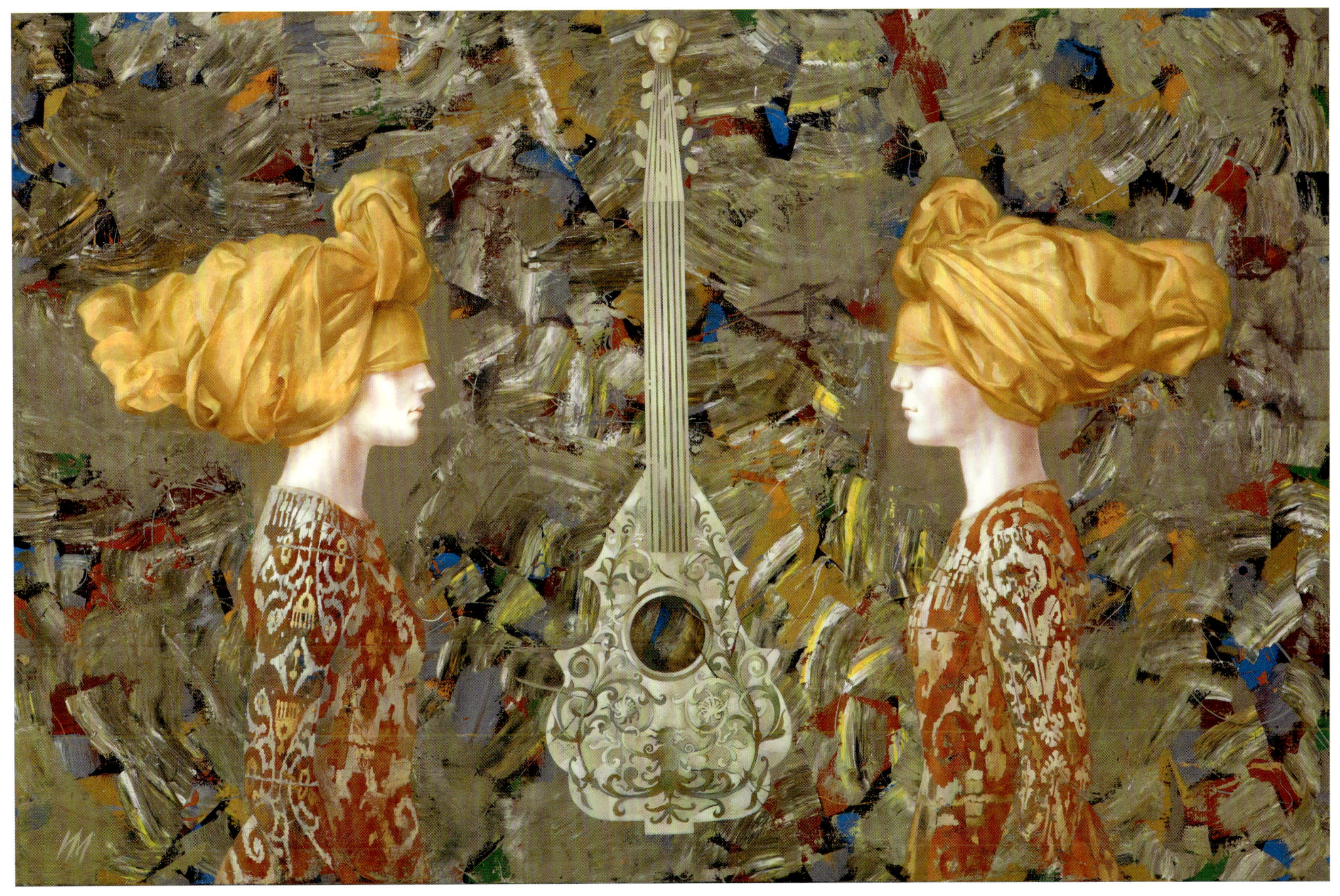

HANDLE WITH CARE SERIES

Fire Bird, oil on canvas, 32 × 52"
(81 × 132 cm)

Red Head, oil on canvas, 64 × 48"
(163 × 122 cm)

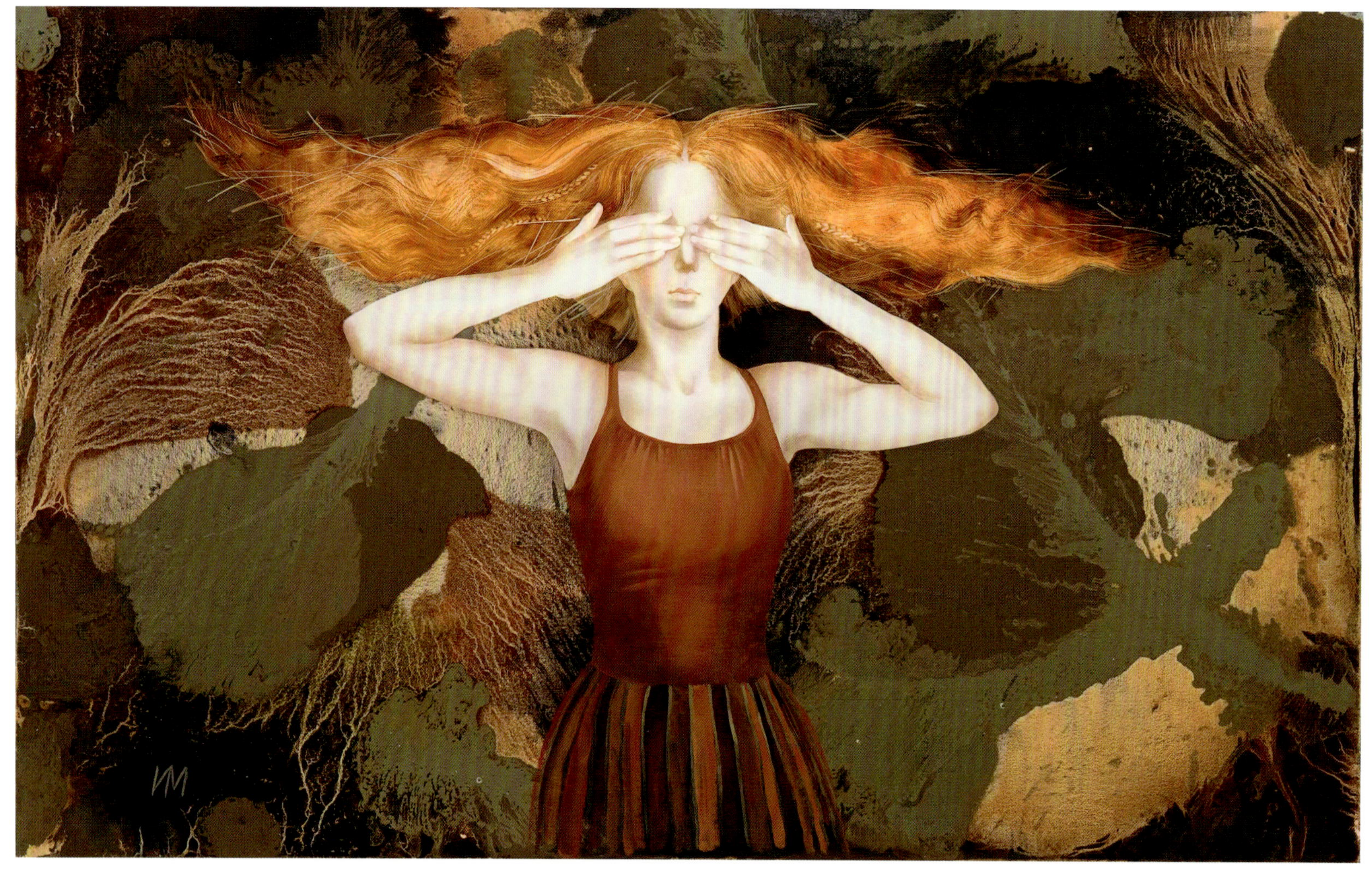

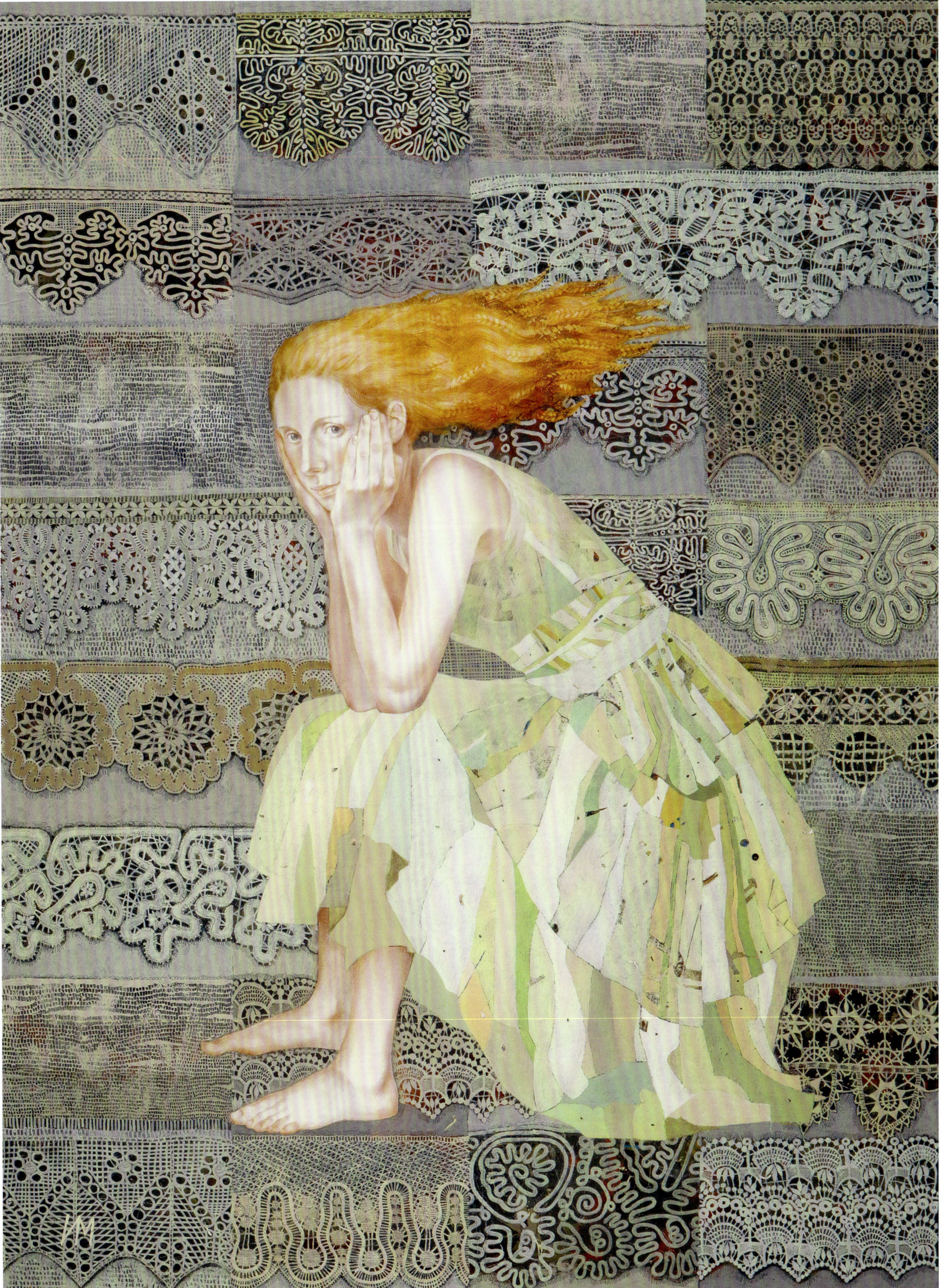

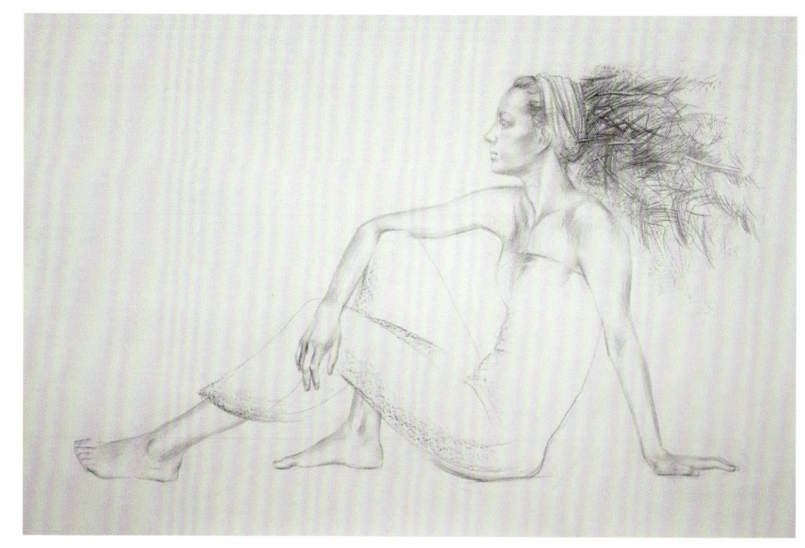

Africa, study, pencil on paper,
48 × 60" (122 × 152 cm)

Africa, oil on canvas,
48 × 60" (122 × 152 cm)

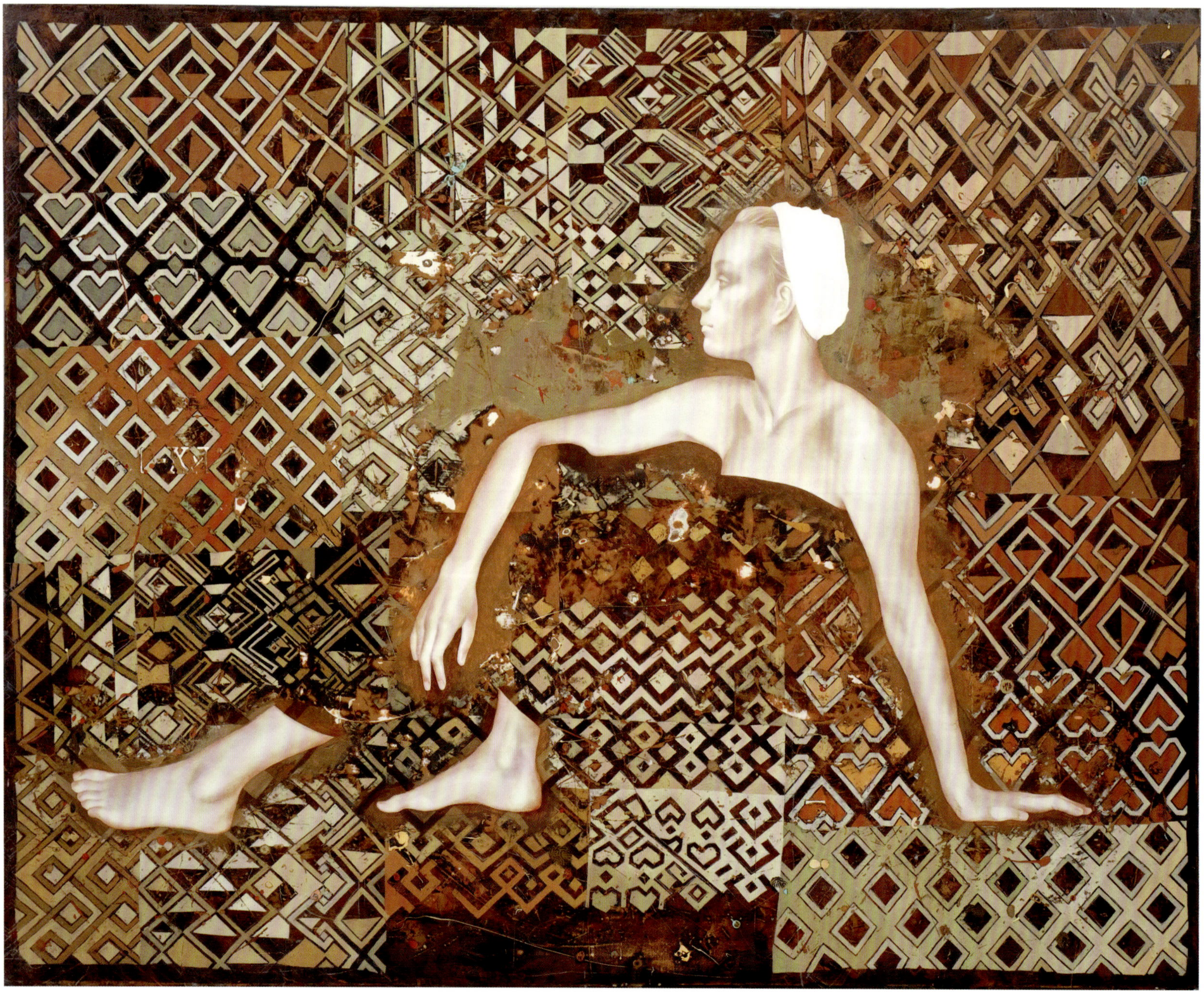

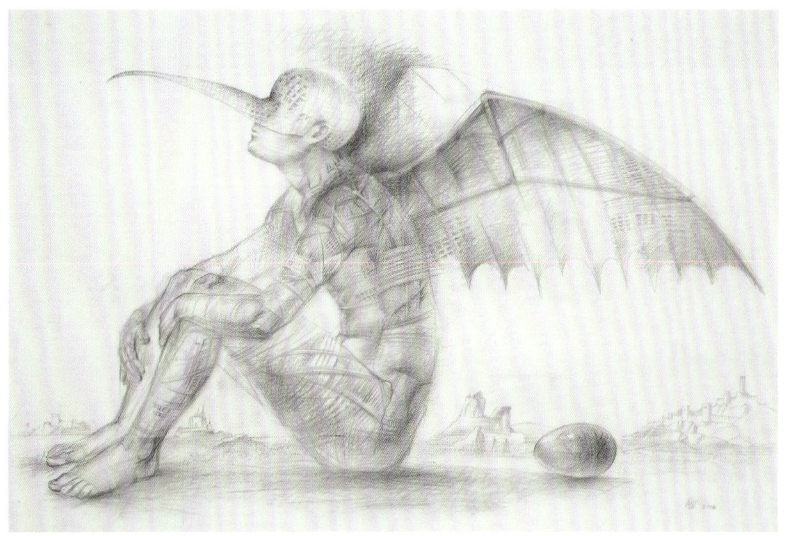

Dreaming Angel, study, pencil on paper,
30 × 40" (76 × 102 cm)

Twelve Apples, oil on canvas, 54 × 72"
(138 × 183 cm)

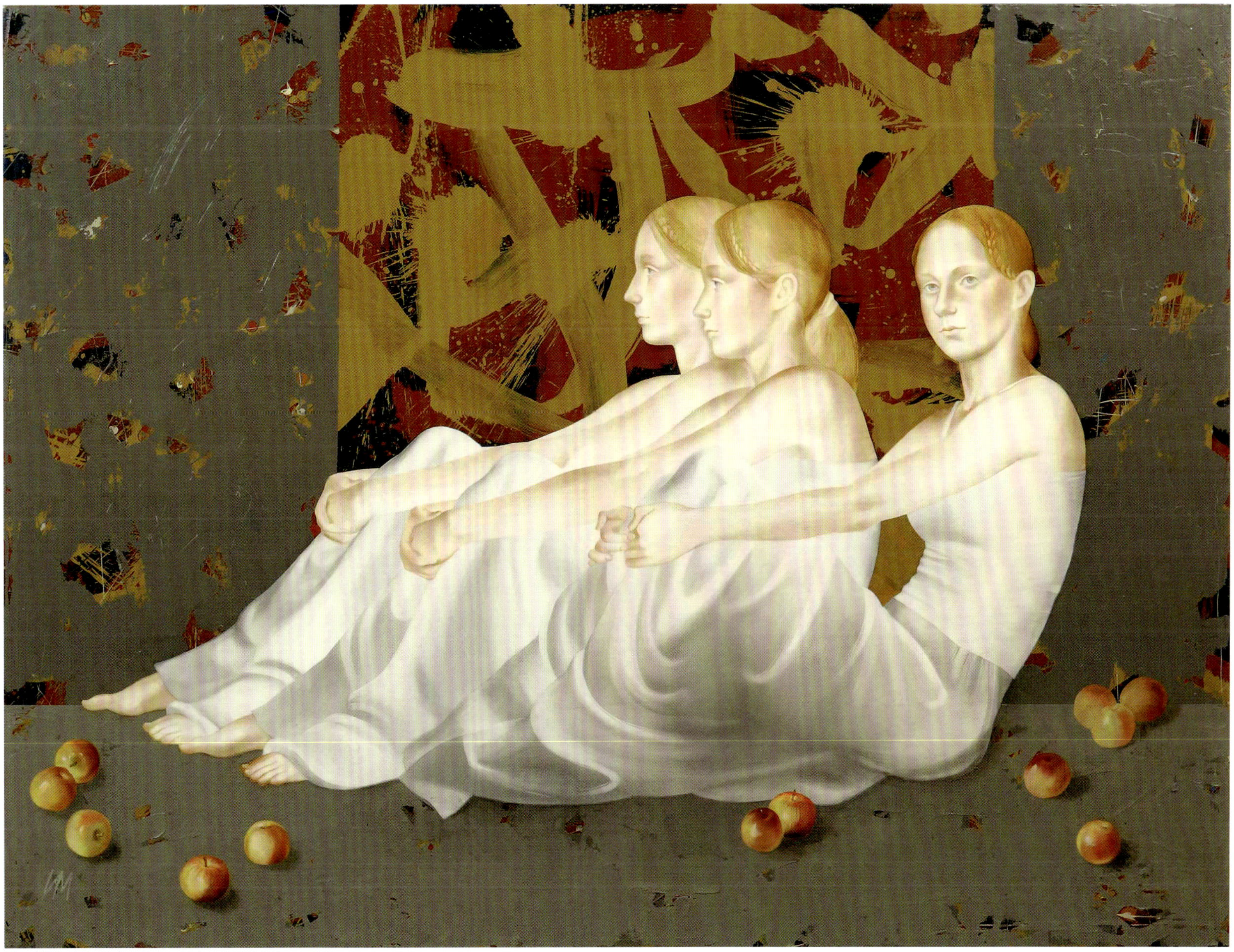

MASQUERADE IS OVER SERIES

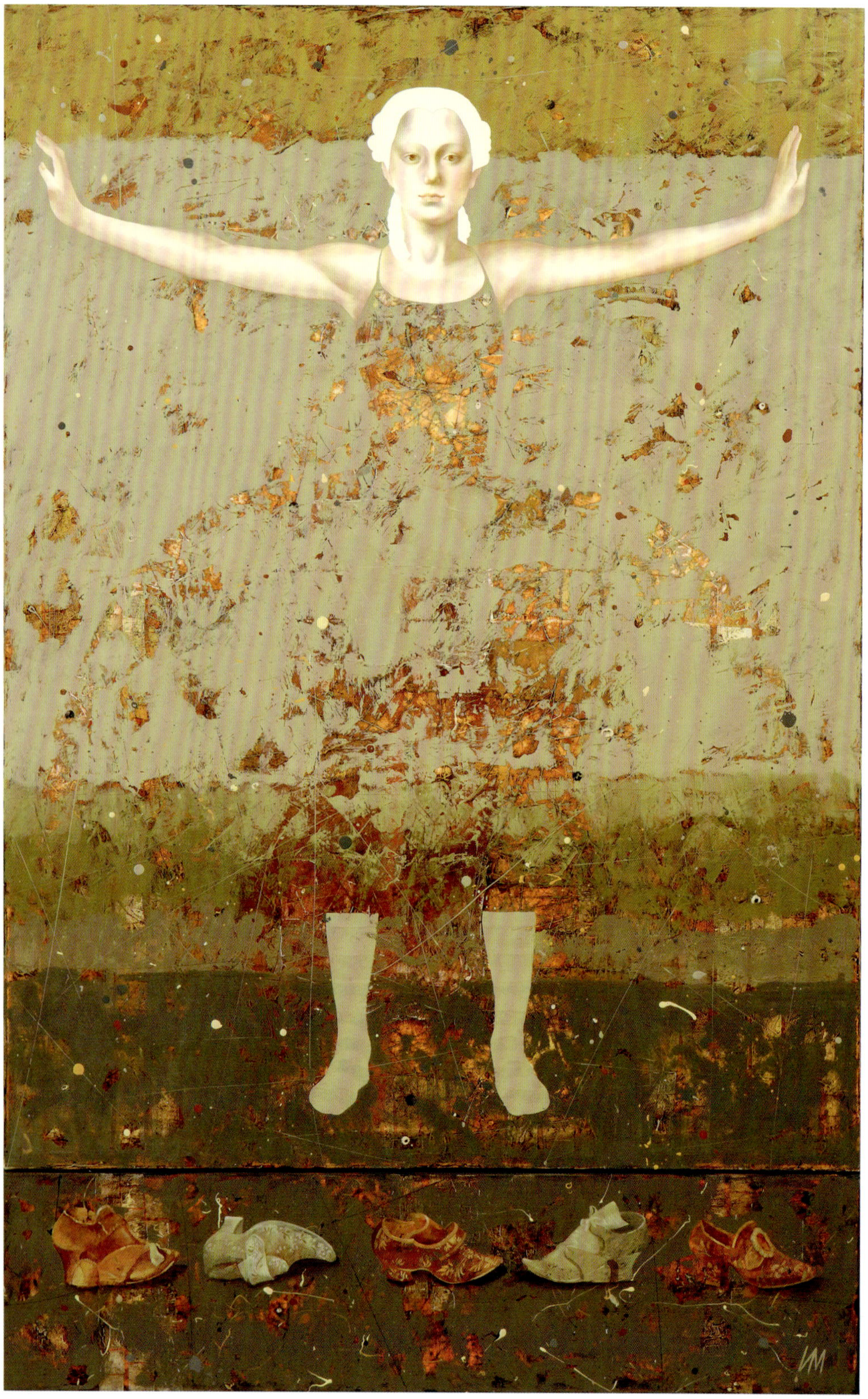

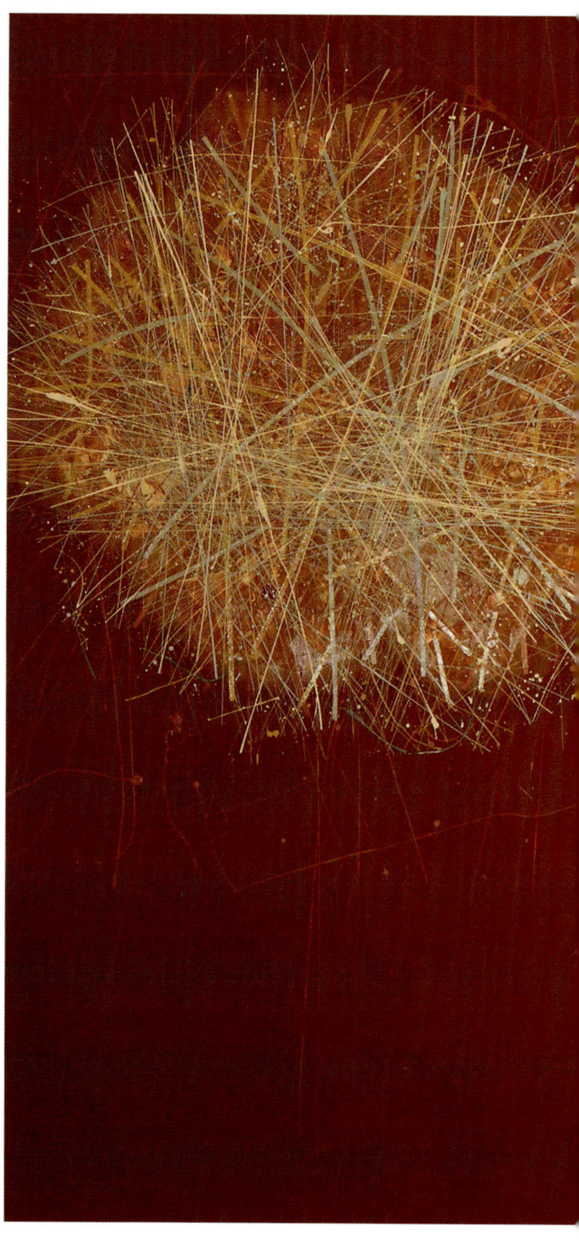

Why Bother with Shoes? (diptych),
oil on canvas, 75 × 48″ (191 × 122 cm)

Regina (triptych), oil on canvas, 48 × 92″
(122 × 234 cm)

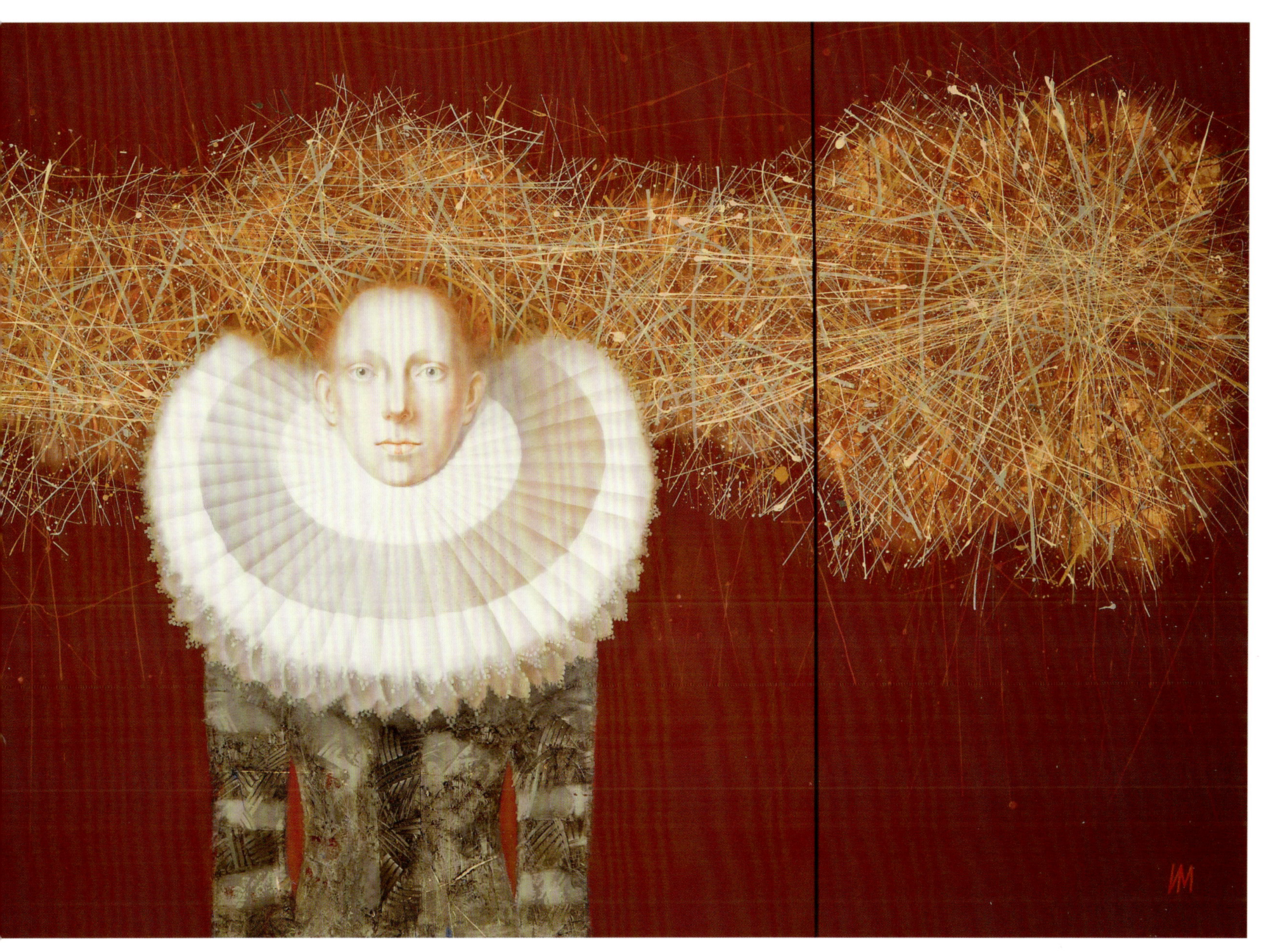

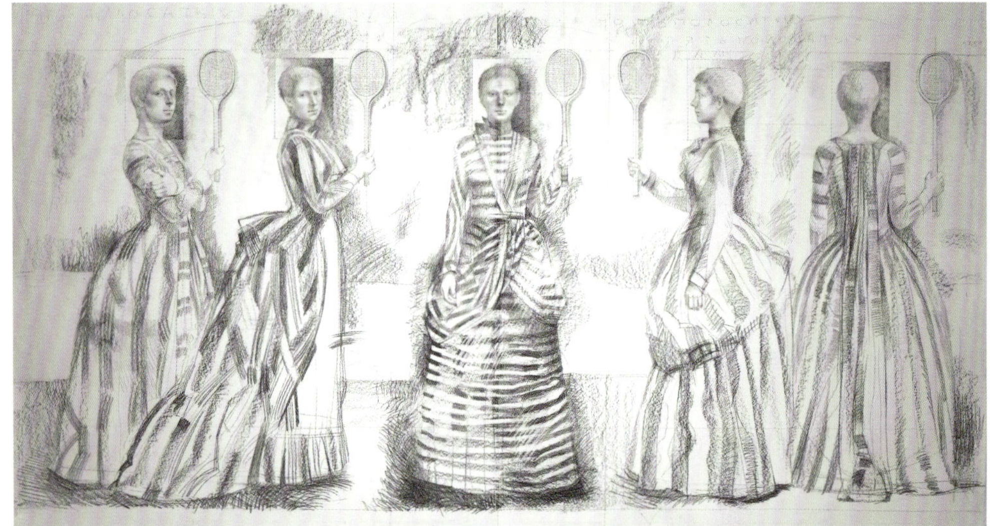

Five Striped Ladies (triptych), study, drawing, pencil on paper, 64 × 122″ (163 × 310 cm)

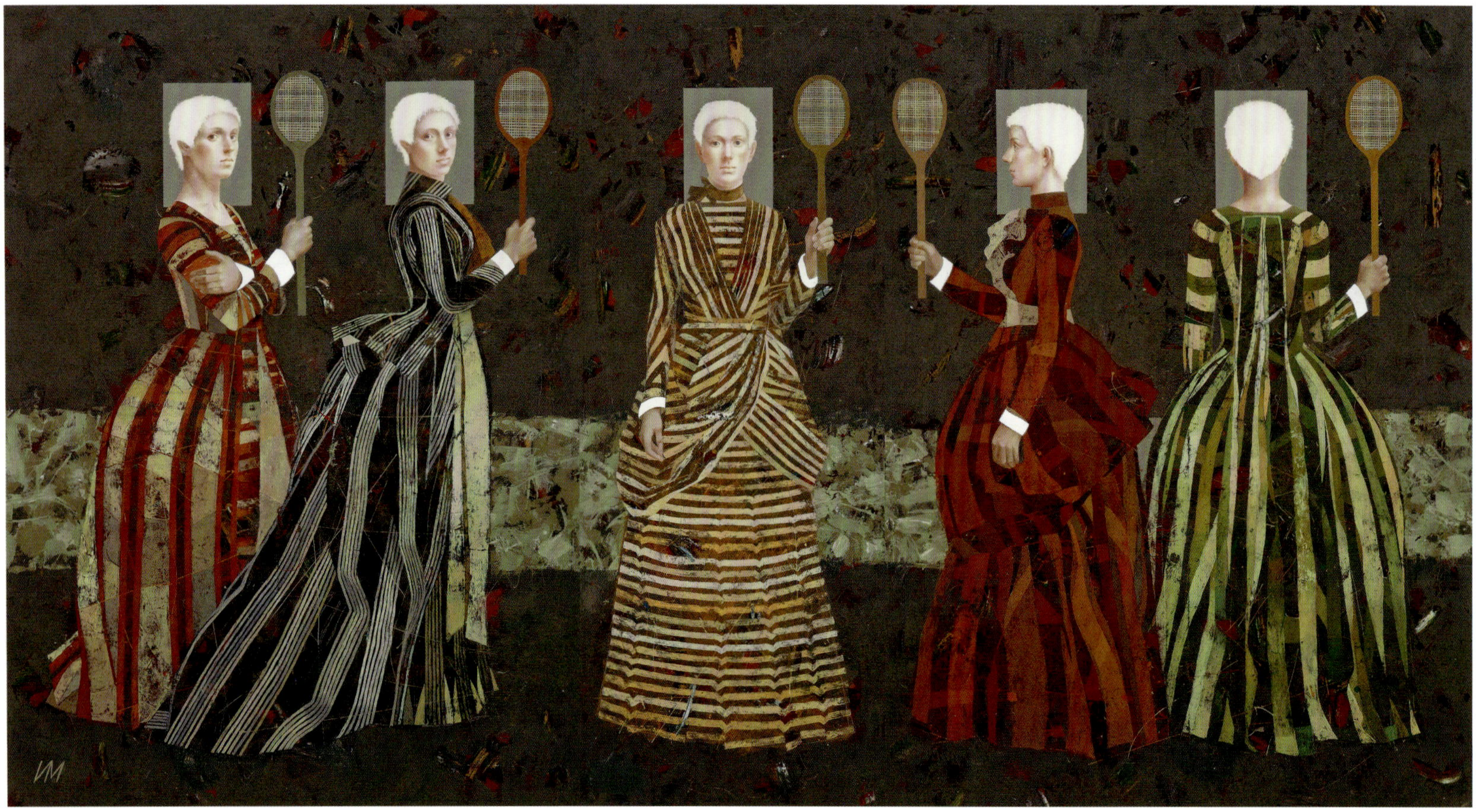

Five Striped Ladies (triptych), oil on canvas, 64 × 122″ (163 × 310 cm)

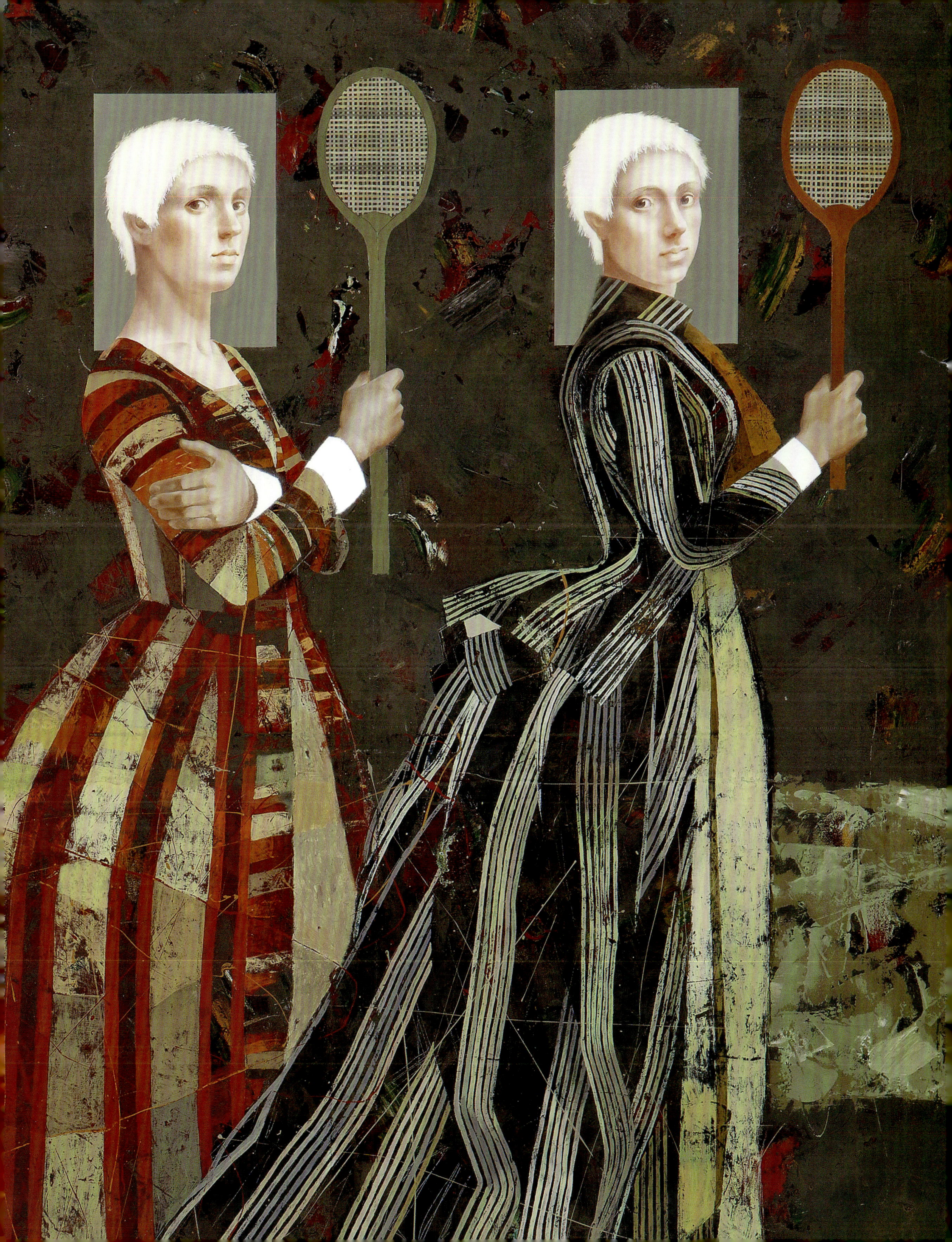

Masquerade is Over, oil on canvas, 70 × 58"
(178 × 147 cm)

Madrid's Court, oil on canvas, 86 × 72"
(218 × 183 cm)

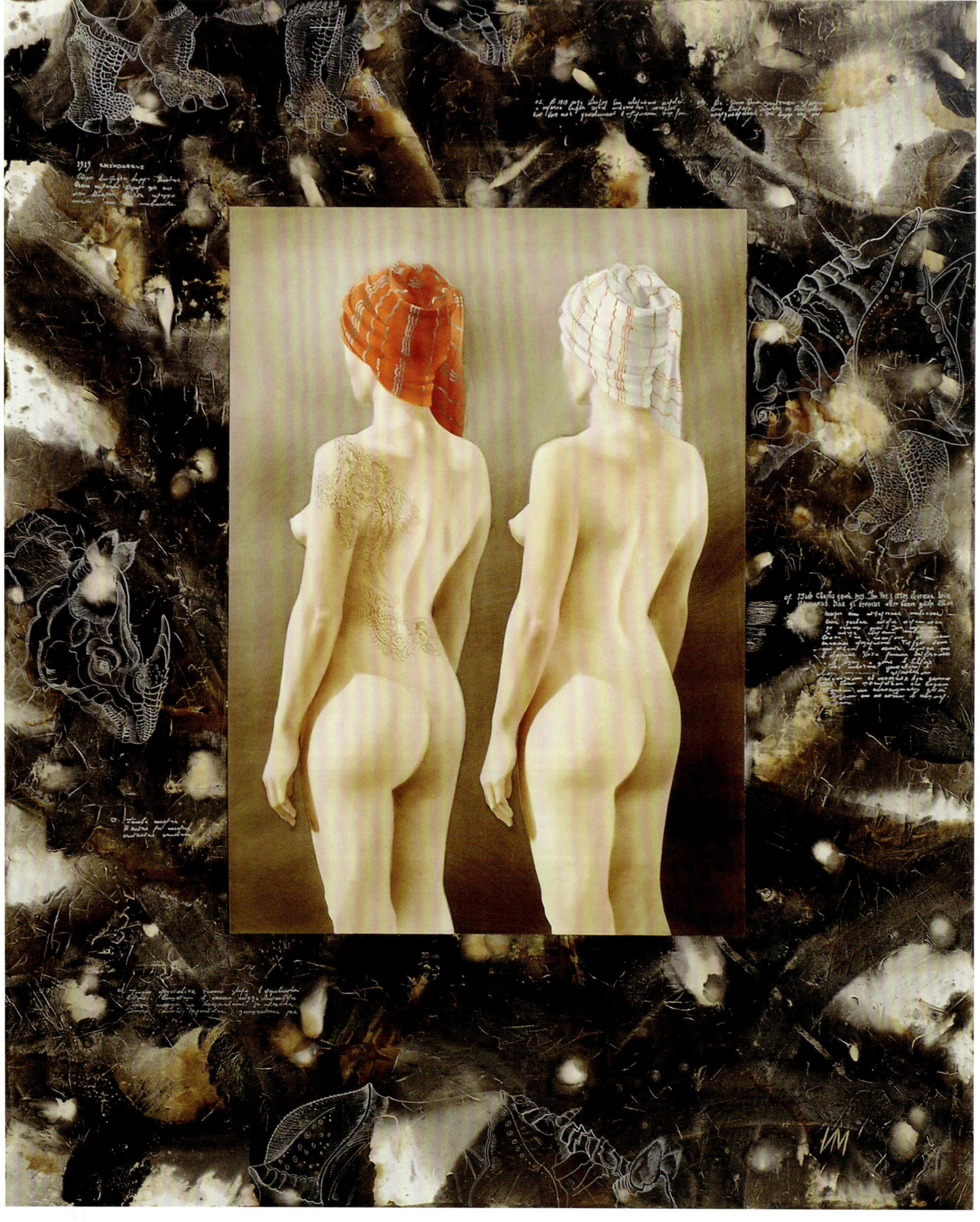

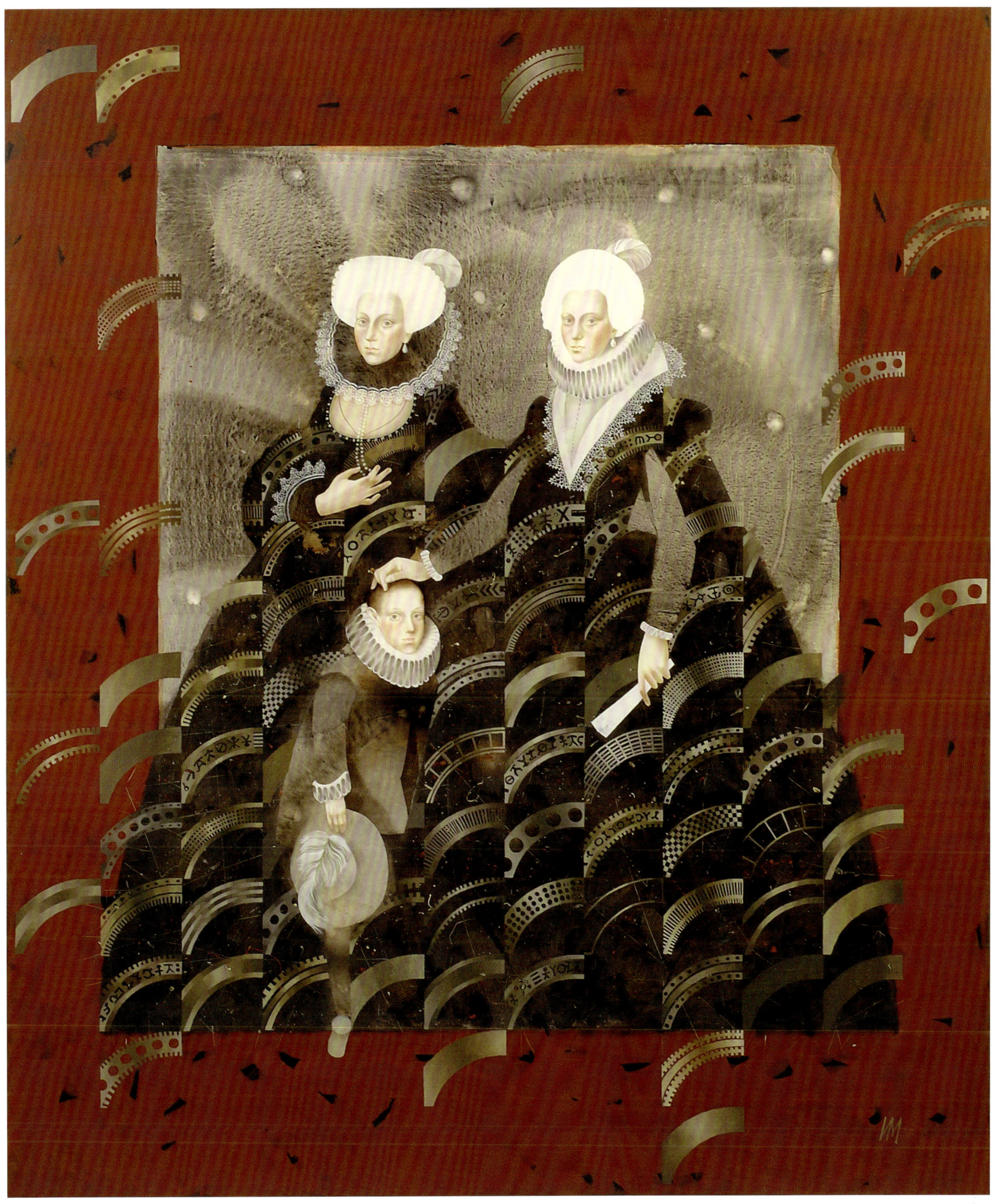

RENAISSANCE THAT NEVER WAS SERIES

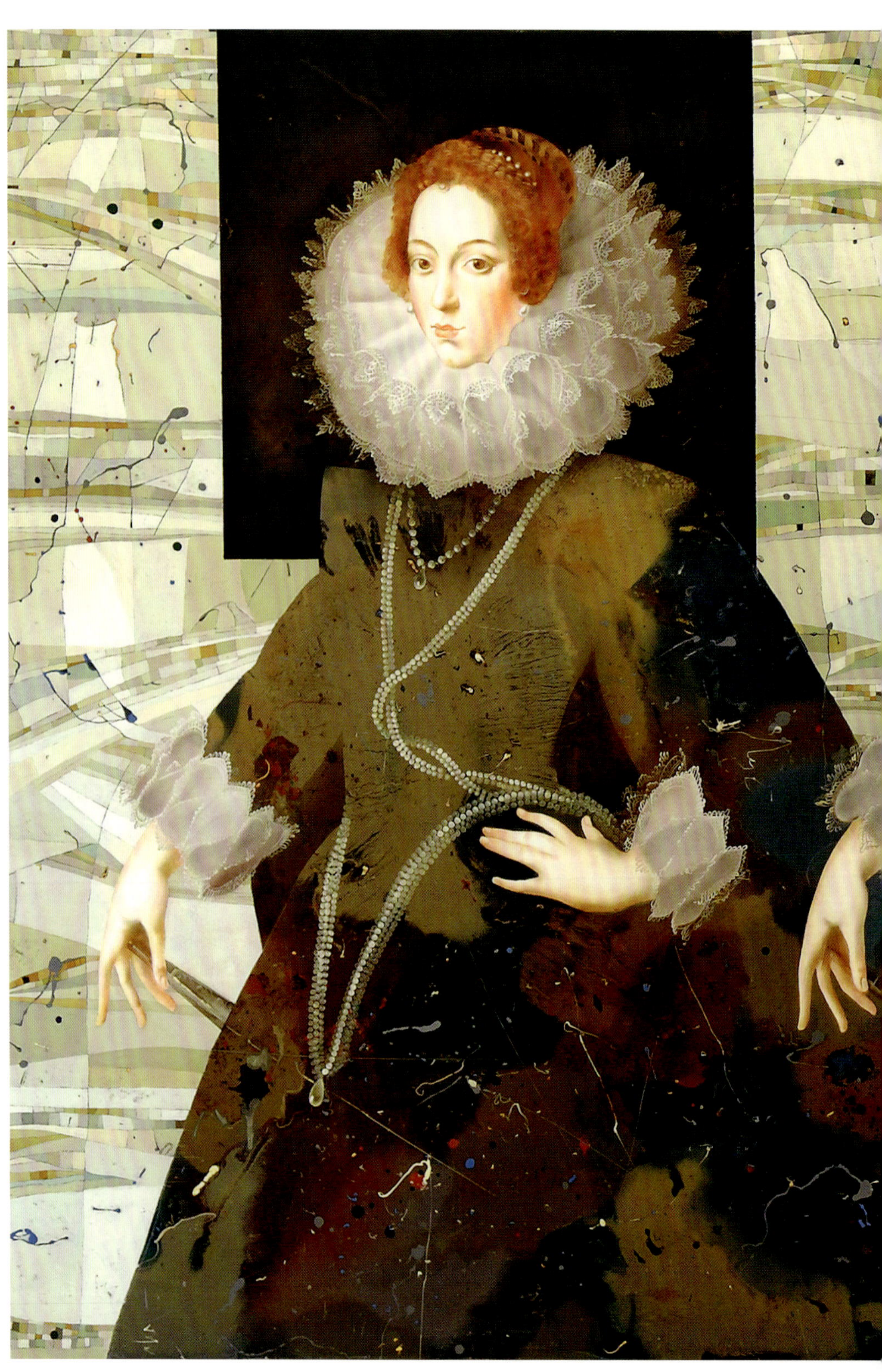

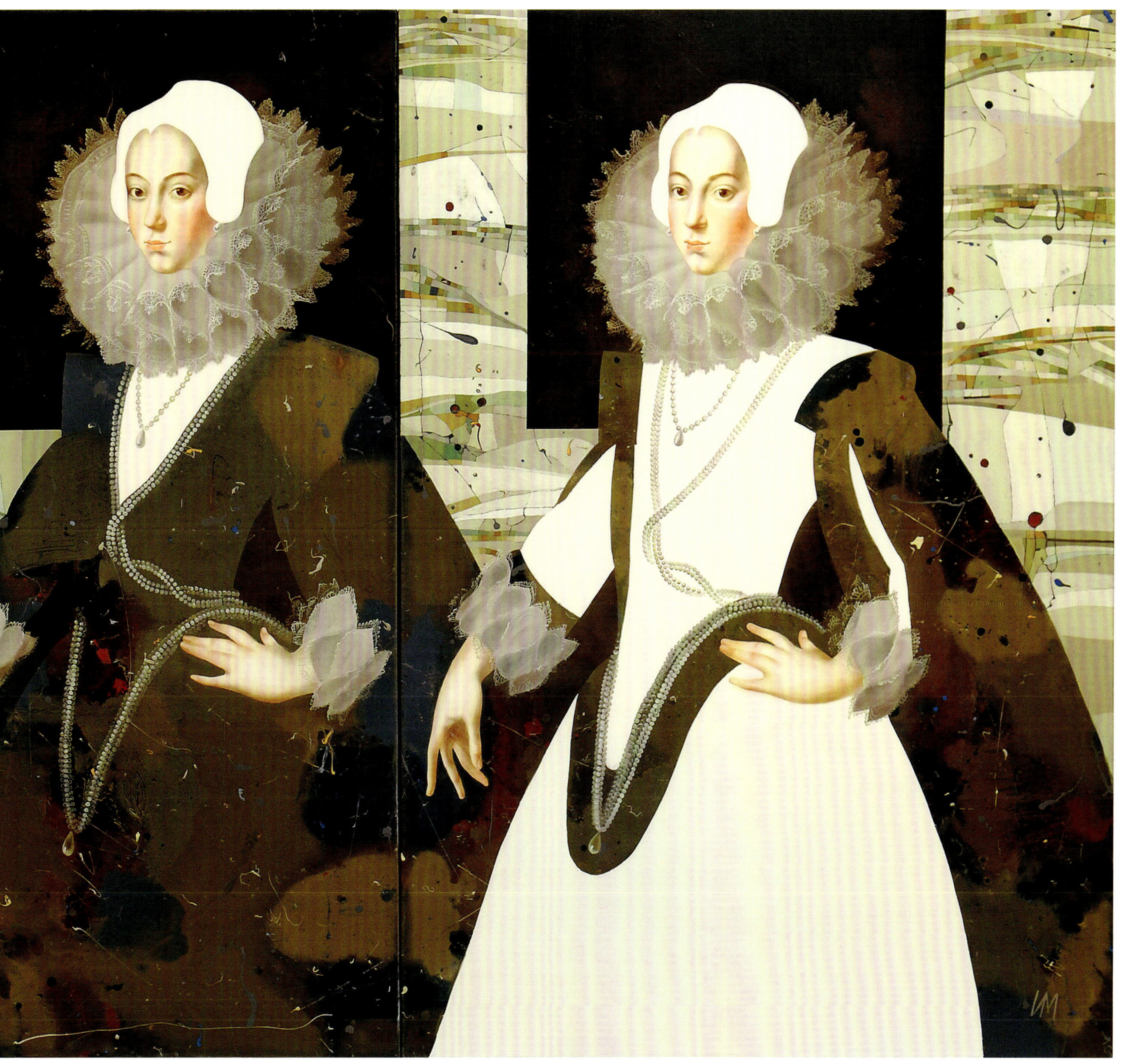

Isabella (triptych), oil on canvas, 68 × 124″
(173 × 315 cm)

Black Hen, study, pencil on paper,
60 × 44″ (152 × 112 cm)

Black Hen, oil on canvas, 72 × 44″
(183 × 112 cm)

Two Heads are Better Than One,
oil on canvas, 60 × 48″ (152 × 122 cm)

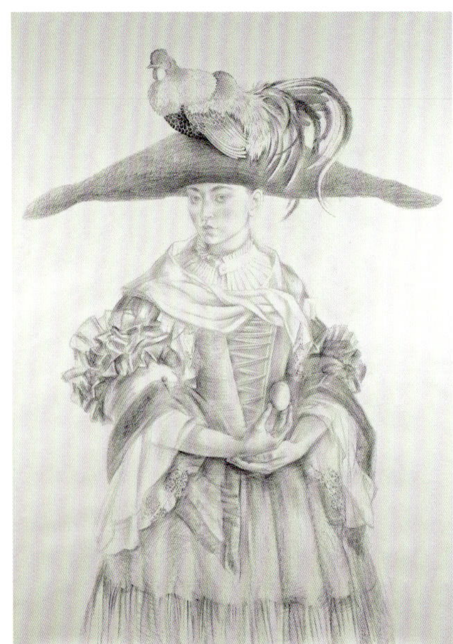

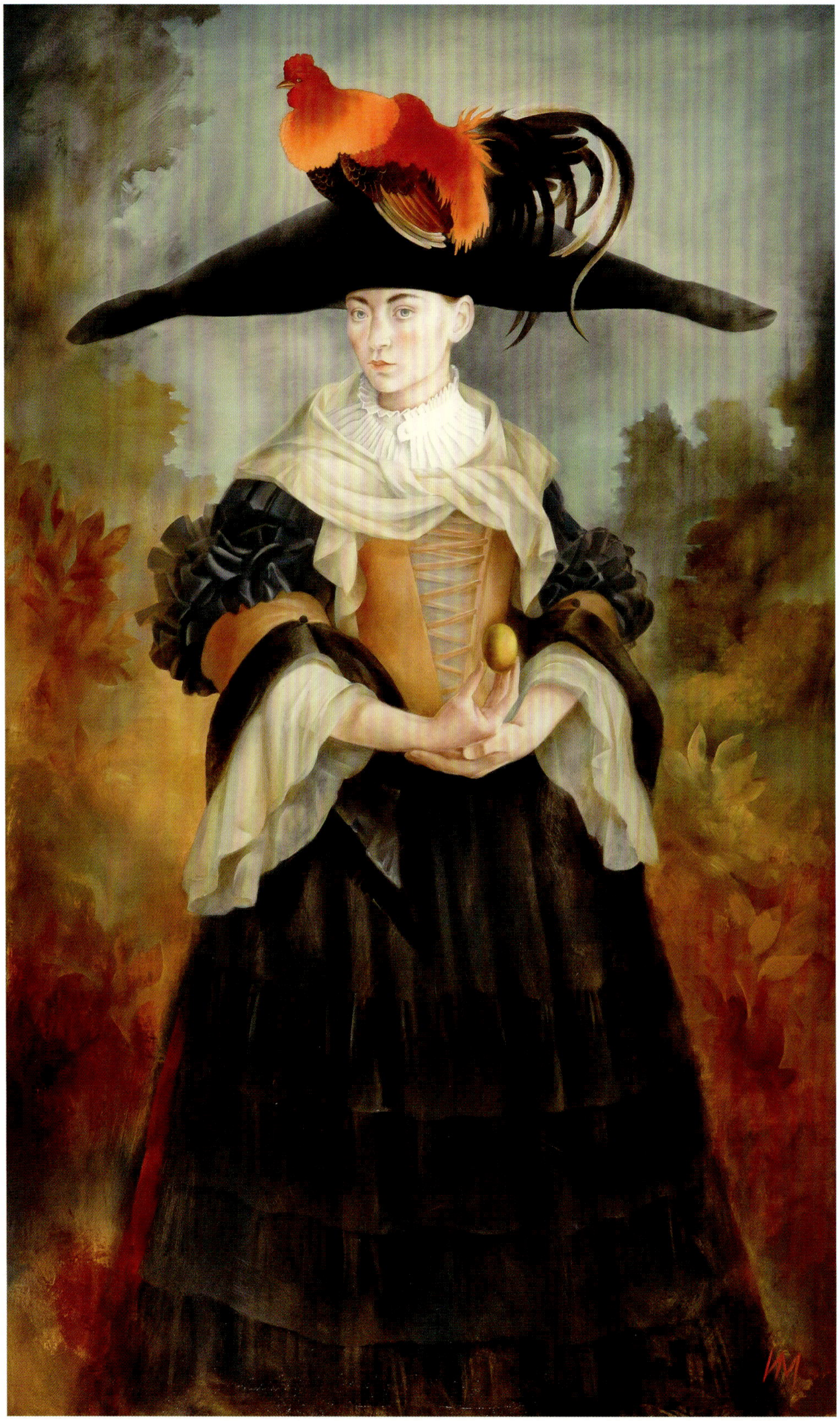

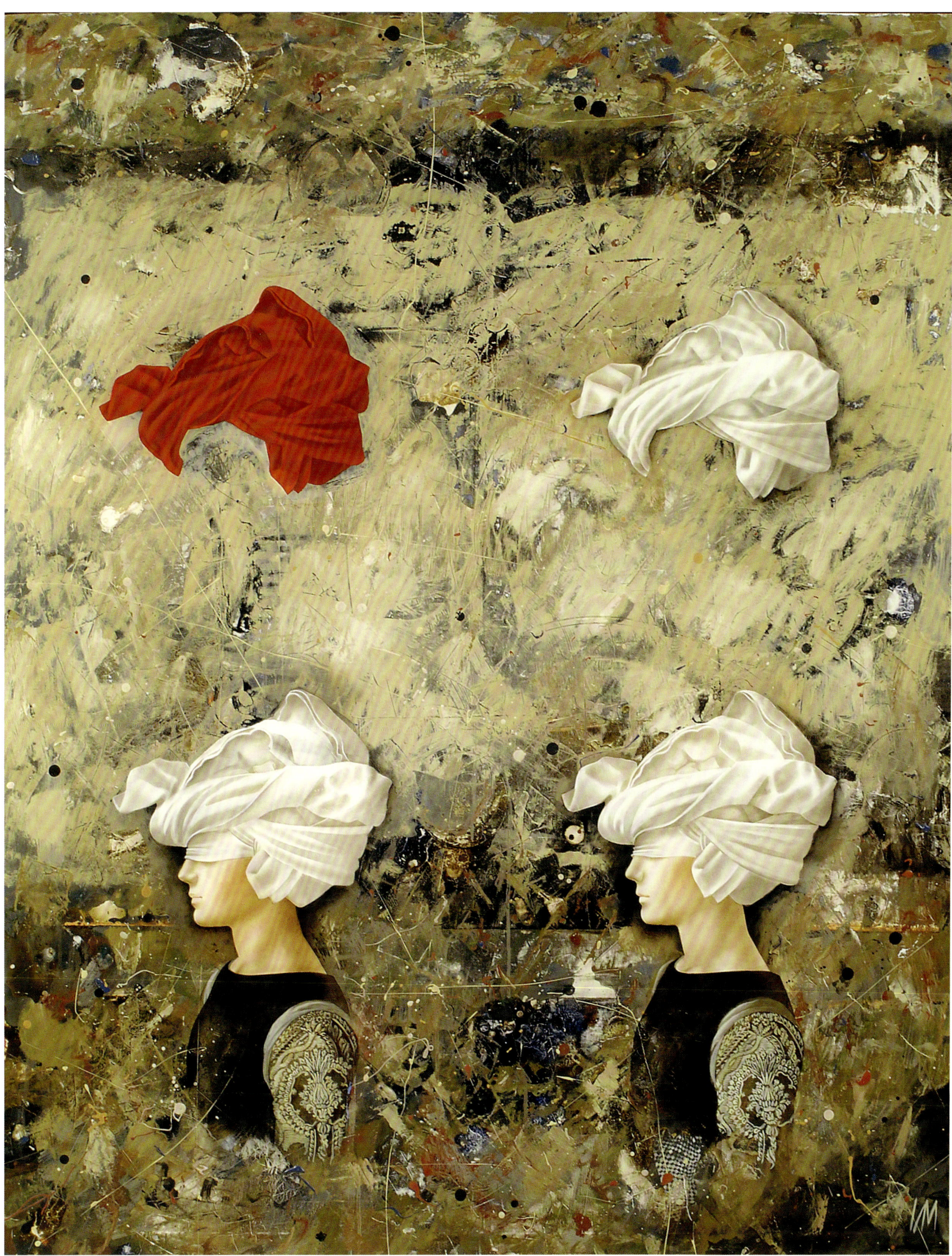

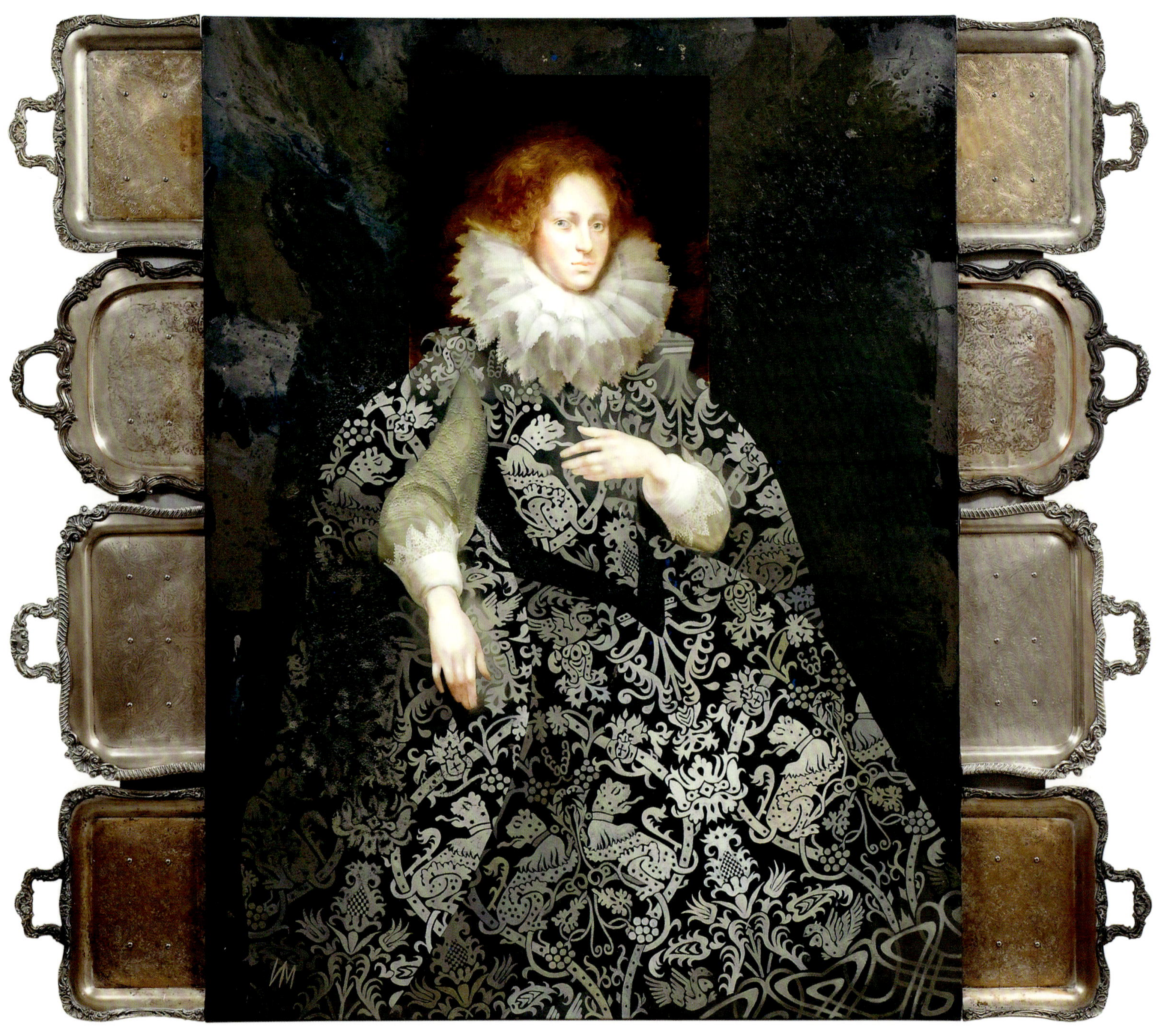

White Nights (triptych), oil on canvas,
antique silver plates, 62 × 72″ (157 × 183 cm)

Copper Queen (diptych), oil on canvas,
copper plate, 44 × 64″ (112 × 163 cm)

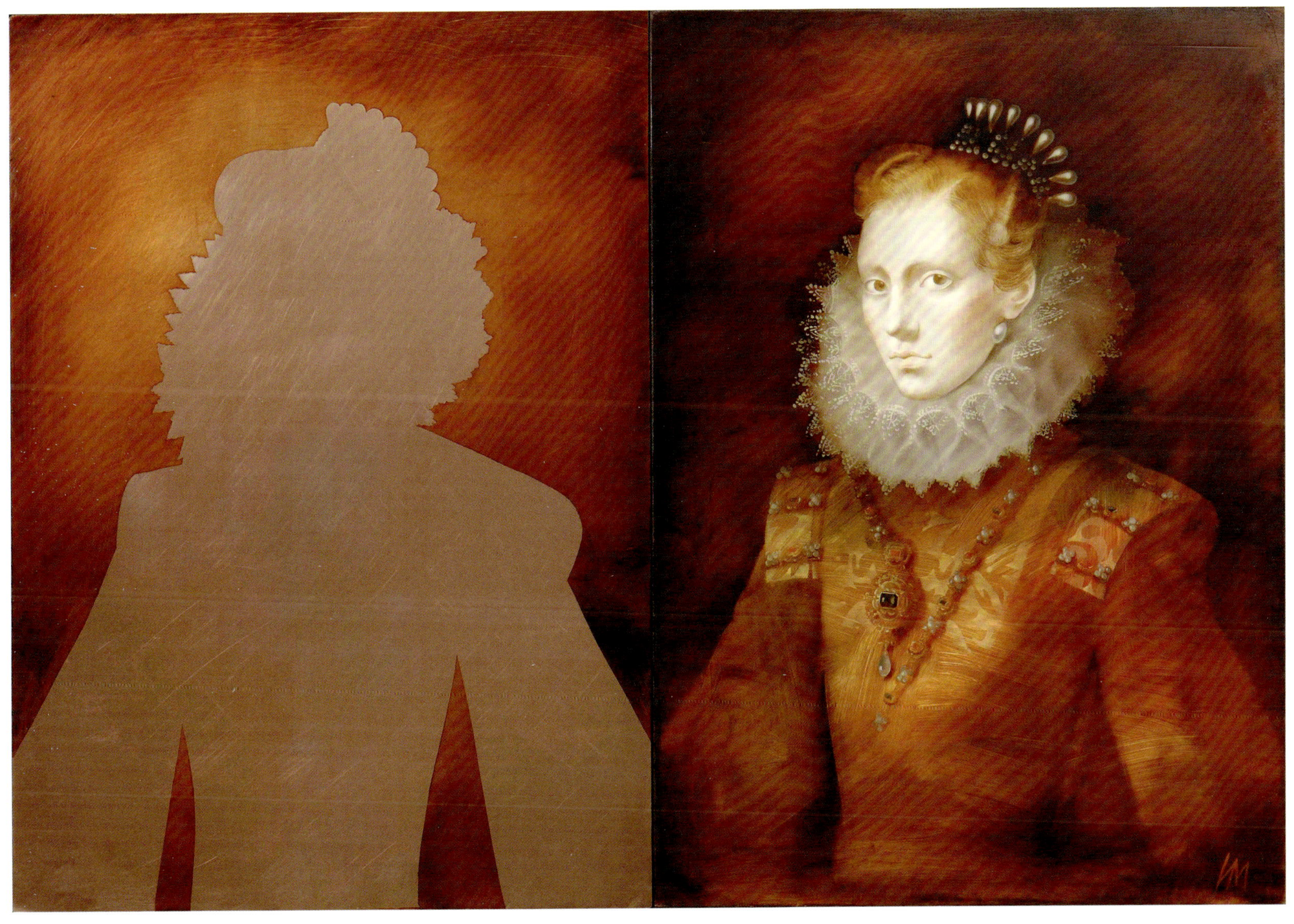

Straw Queen, drawing, pencil on paper,
40 × 30″ (102 × 76 cm)

Air of Time, oil on canvas, 60 × 48″
(152 × 122 cm)

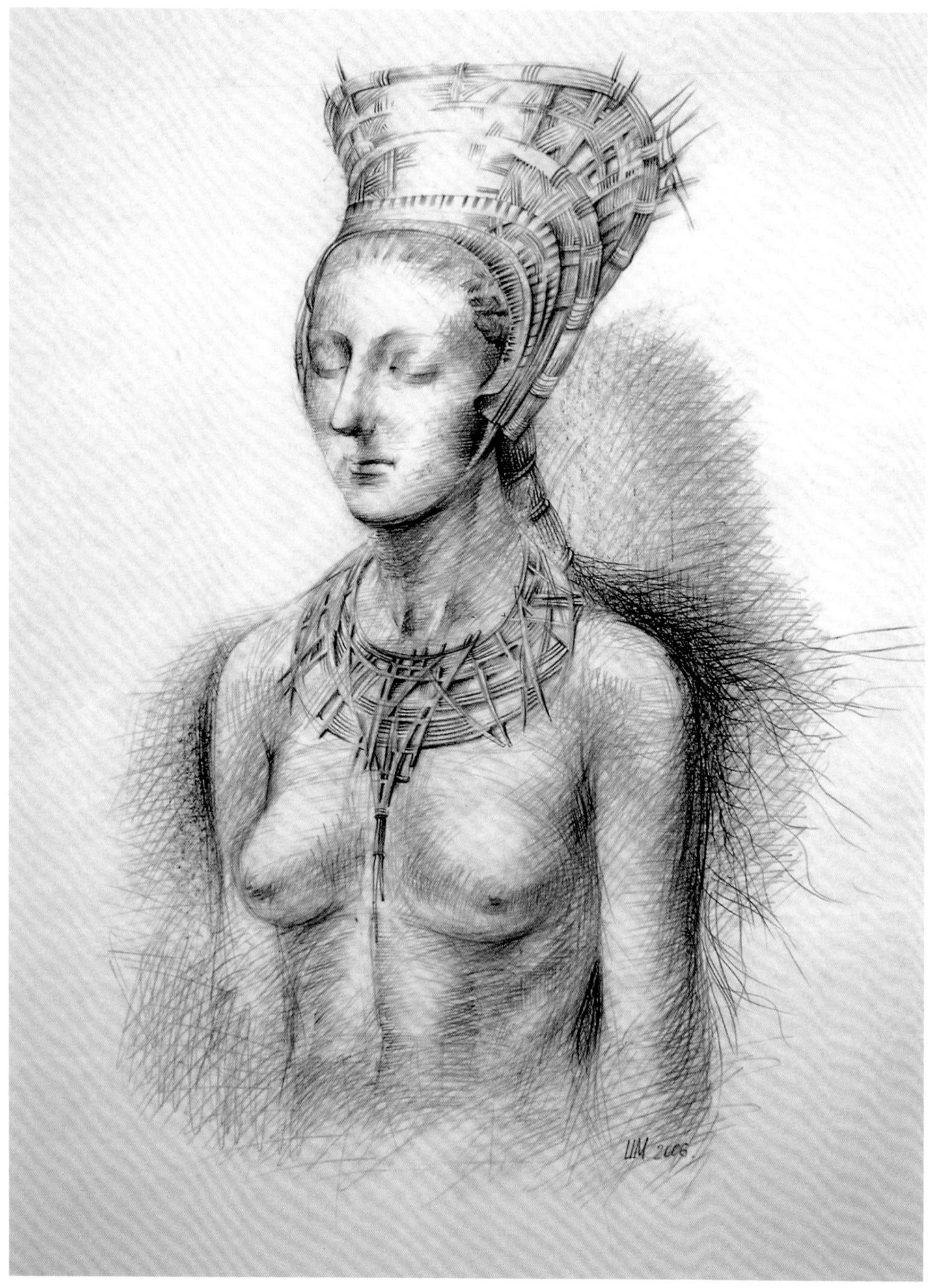

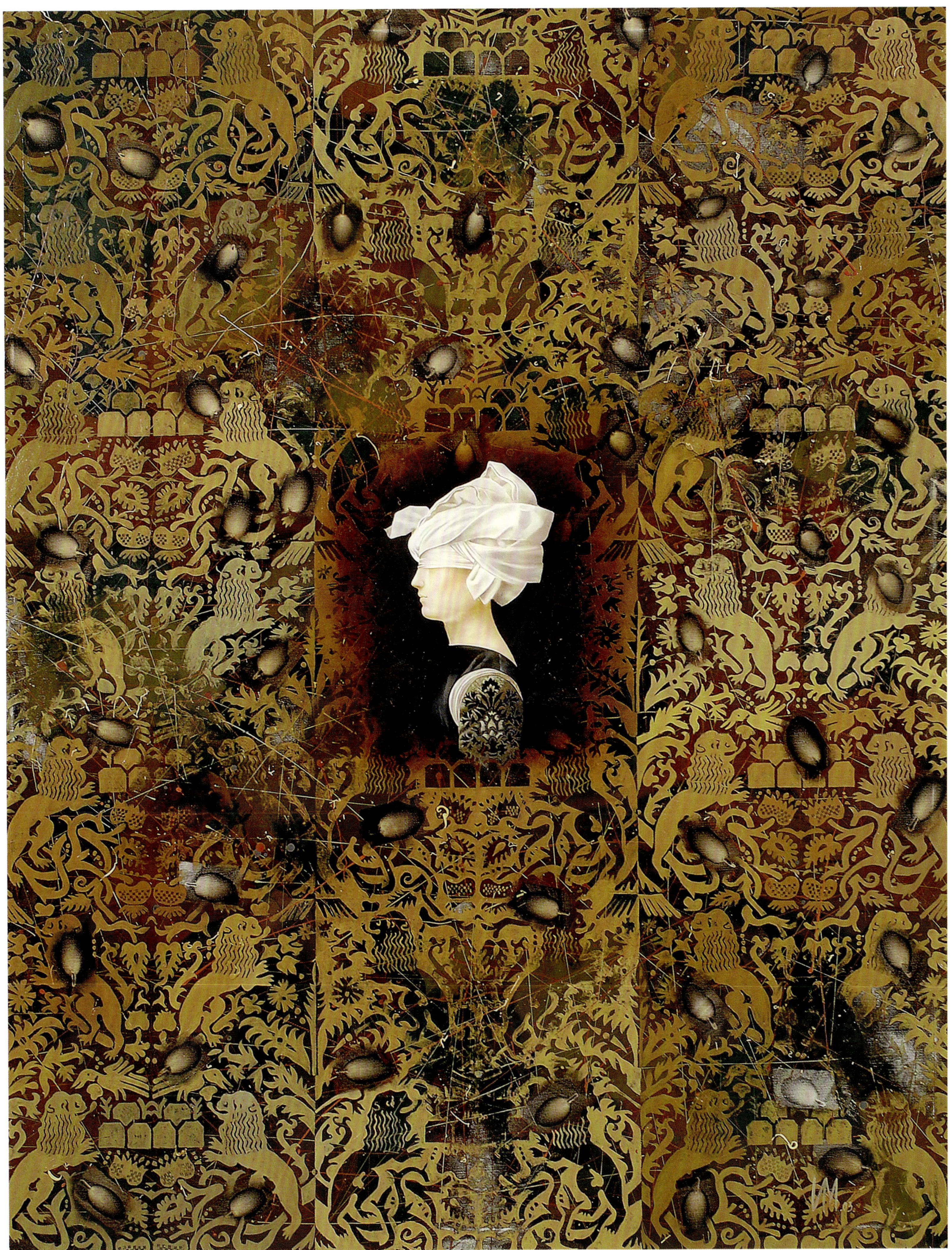

To the Tips of Her Nails, oil on canvas,
58 × 48" (147 × 122 cm)

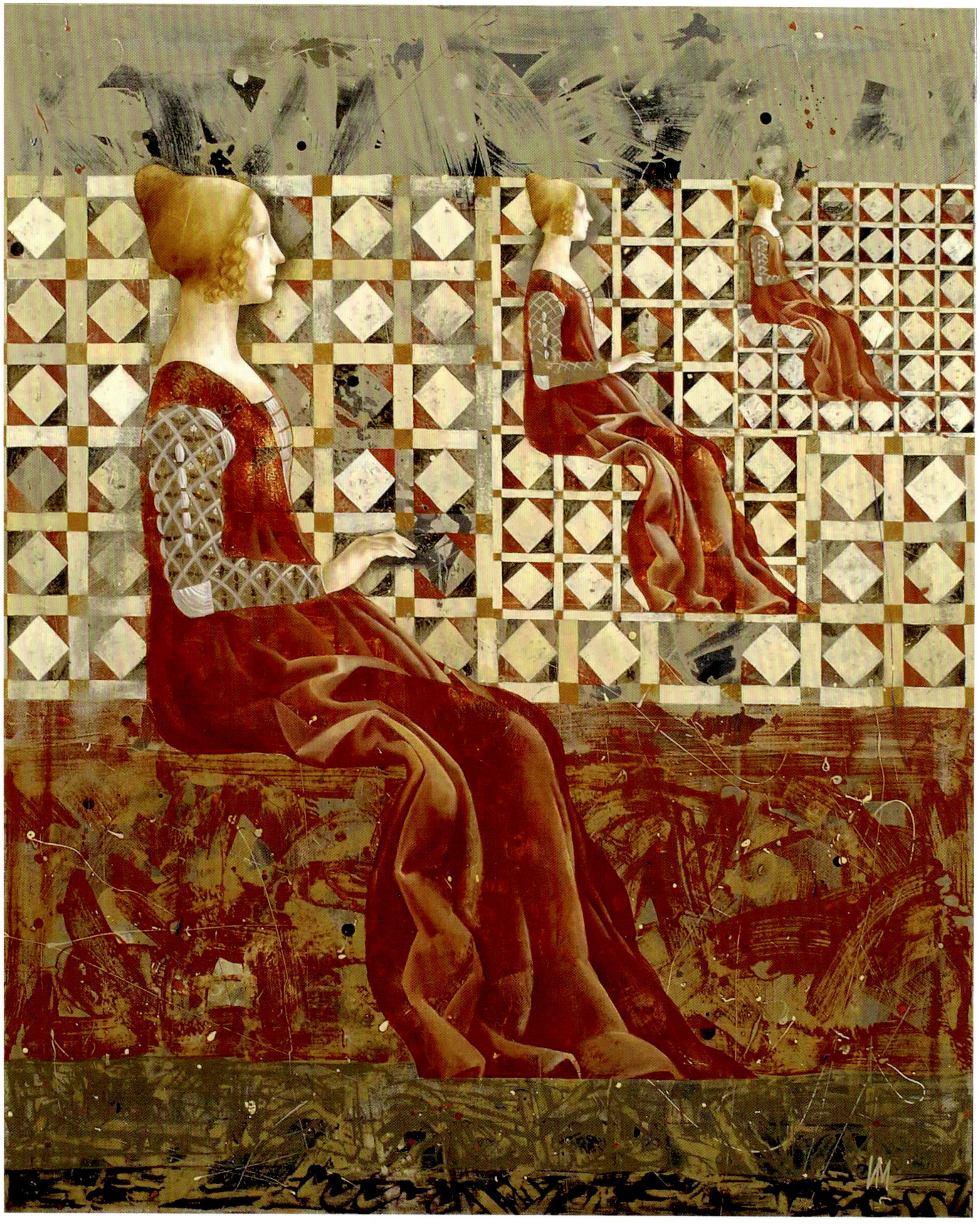

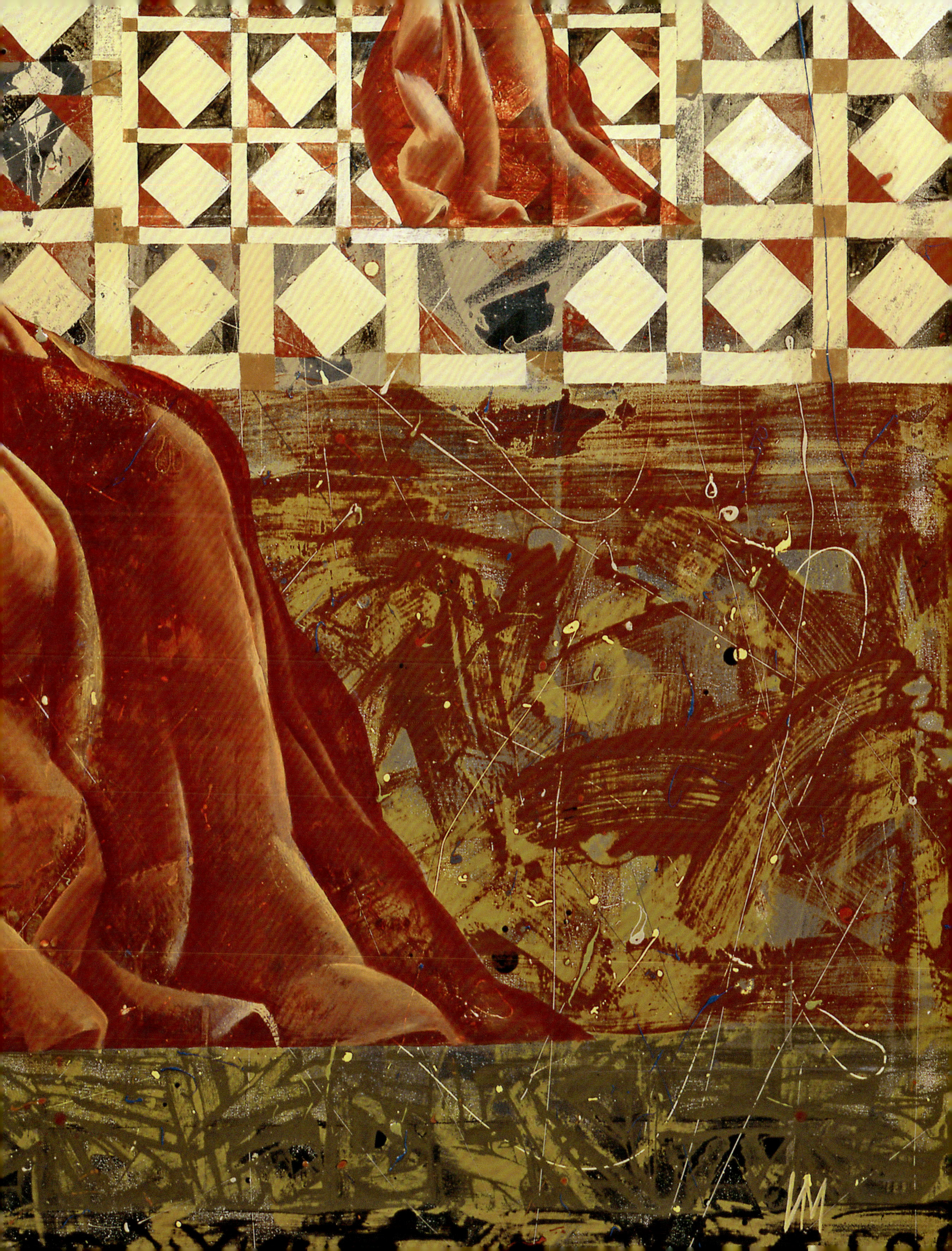

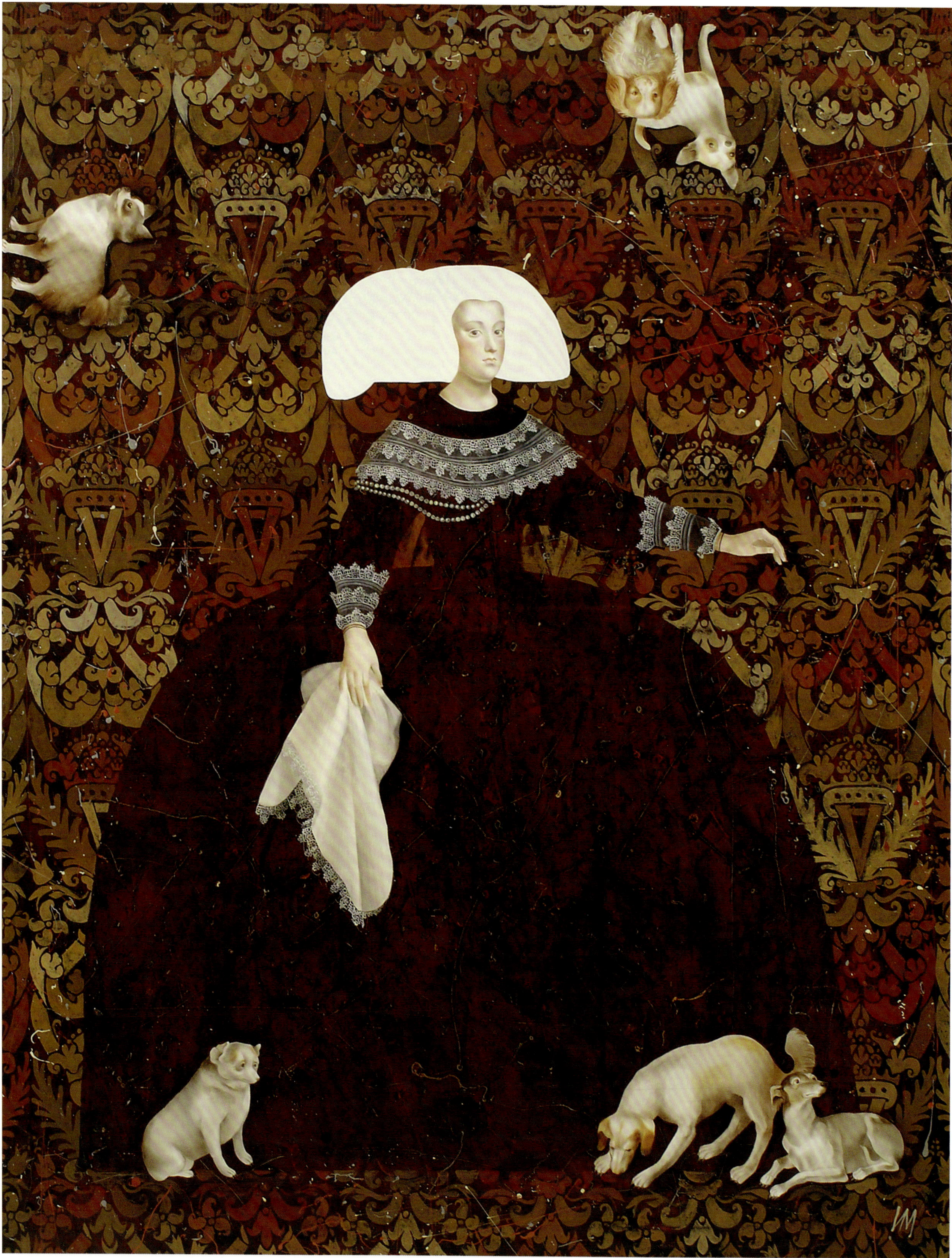

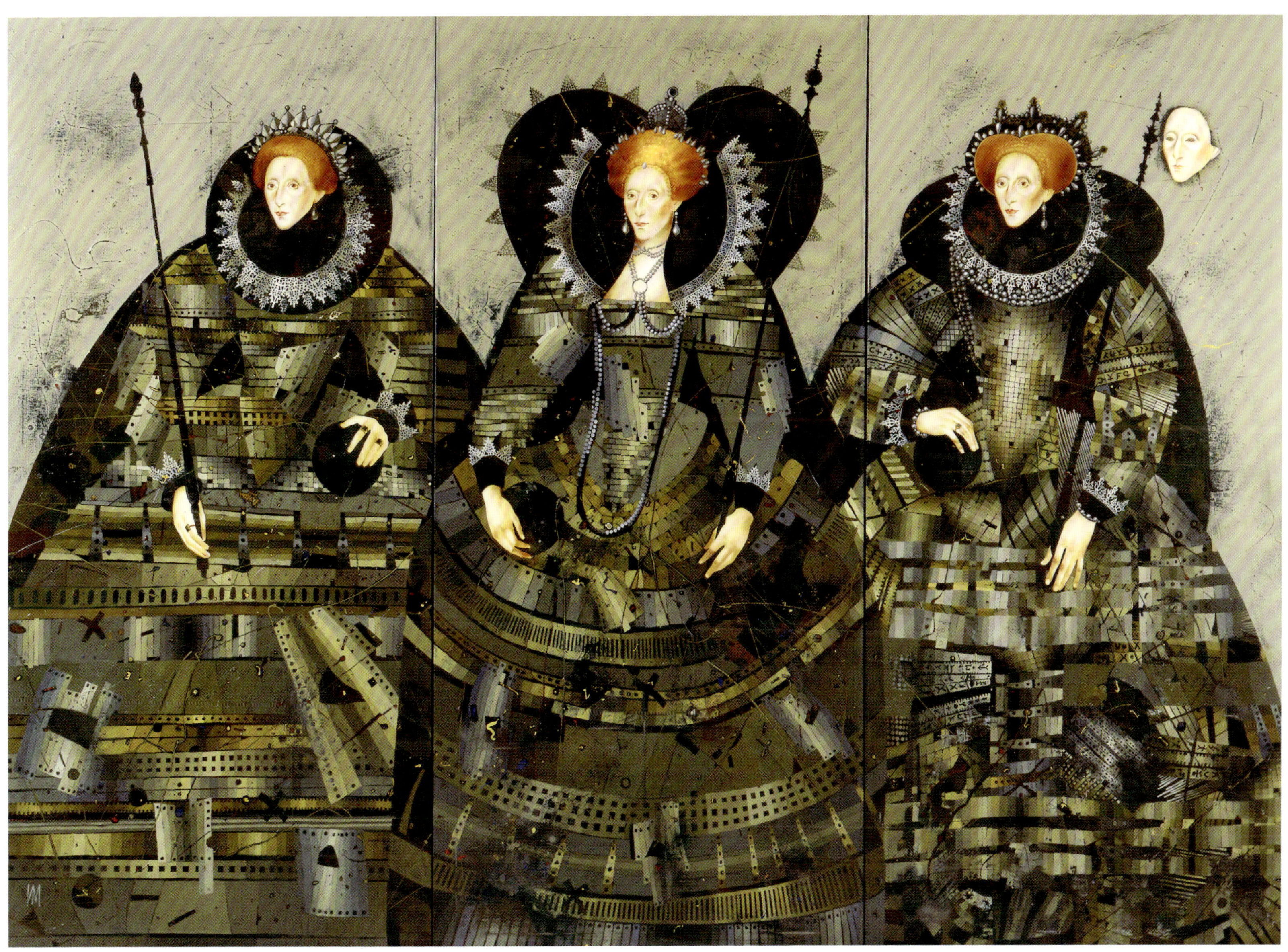

Big Infanta, oil on canvas, 72 × 56″
(183 × 142 cm)

Triple Life of Elizabeth (triptych),
oil on canvas, 79 × 111″ (201 × 282 cm)

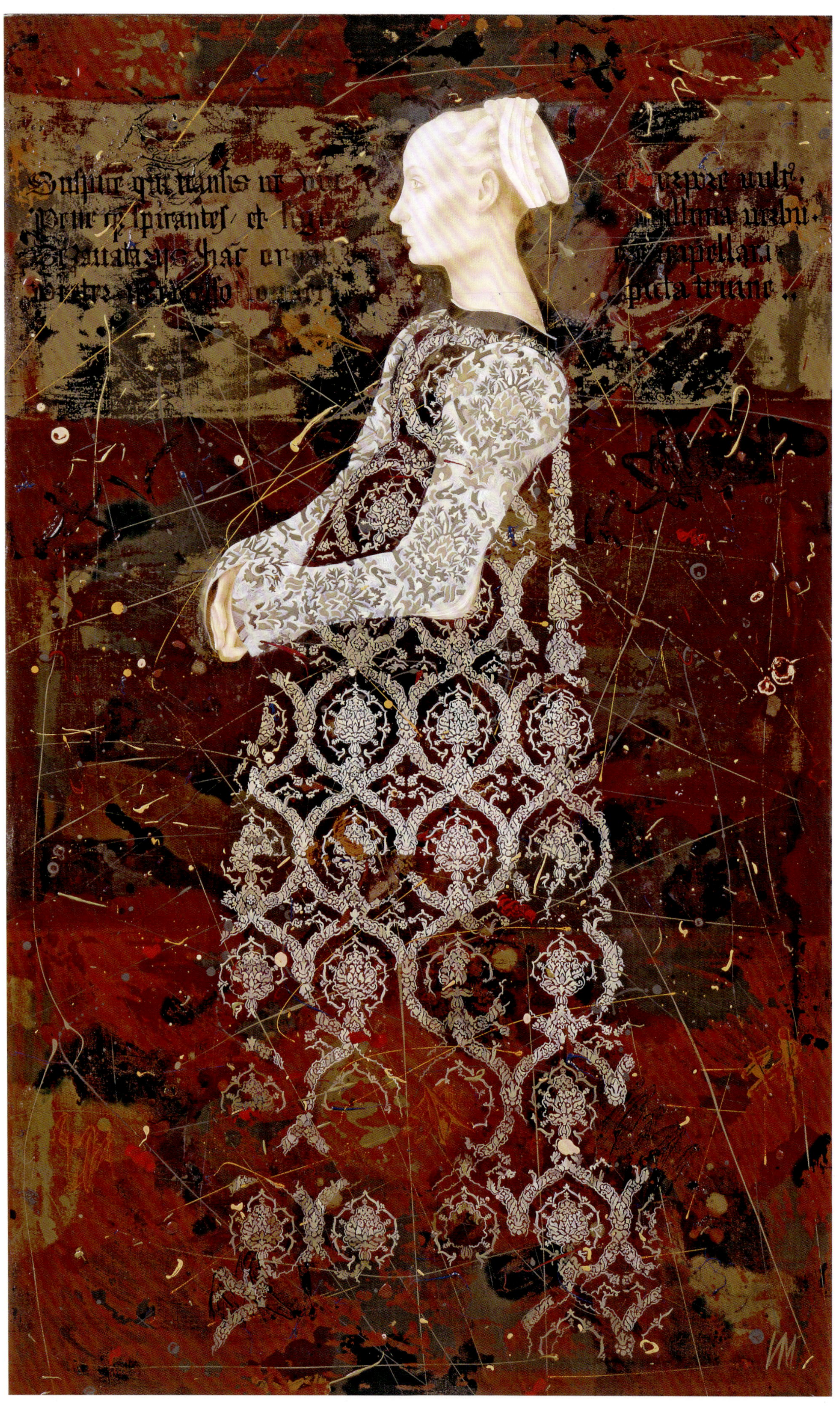

Suspice qui transis ut ...
... me inspirantes et ...
... datibus hac or ...
... tempore vult
... ullima verbu
... puellan
picta trinne ..

Shadow of the Fresco, oil on canvas,
52 × 32″ (132 × 81 cm)

One and a Half Boys in Red, oil on canvas,
60 × 60″ (152 × 152 cm)

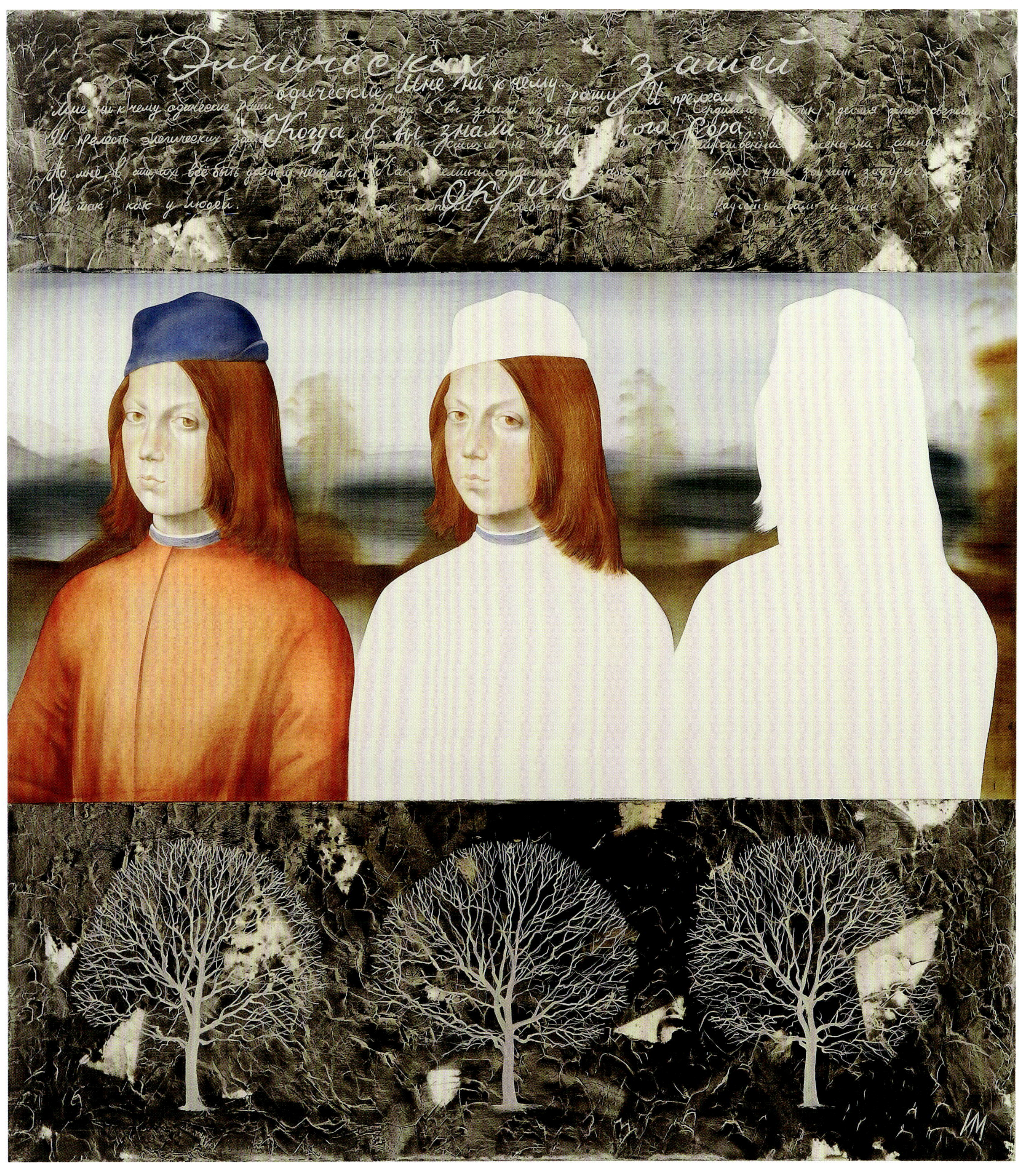

Game, oil on Belgian linen, 30 × 40″
(76 × 102 cm)

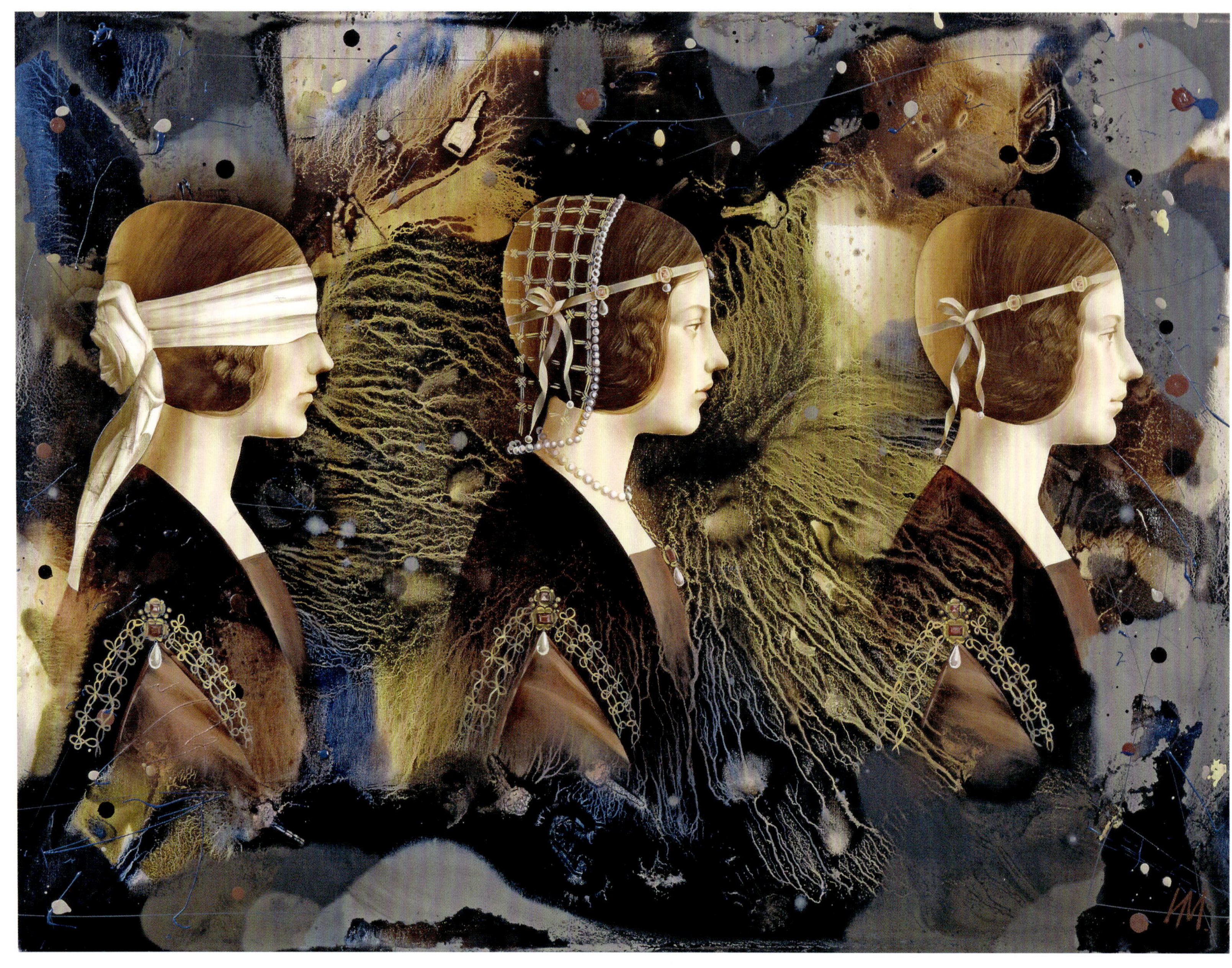

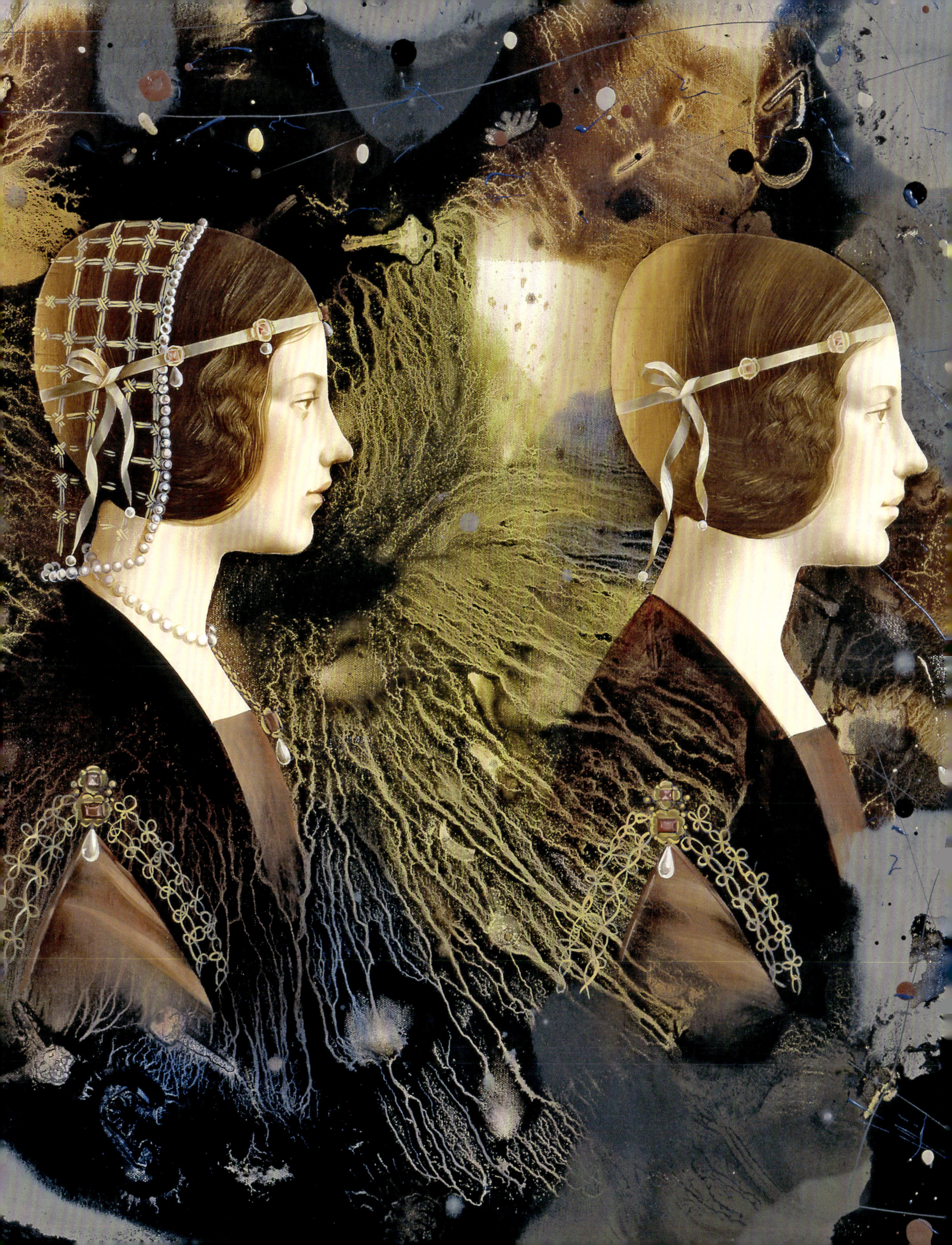

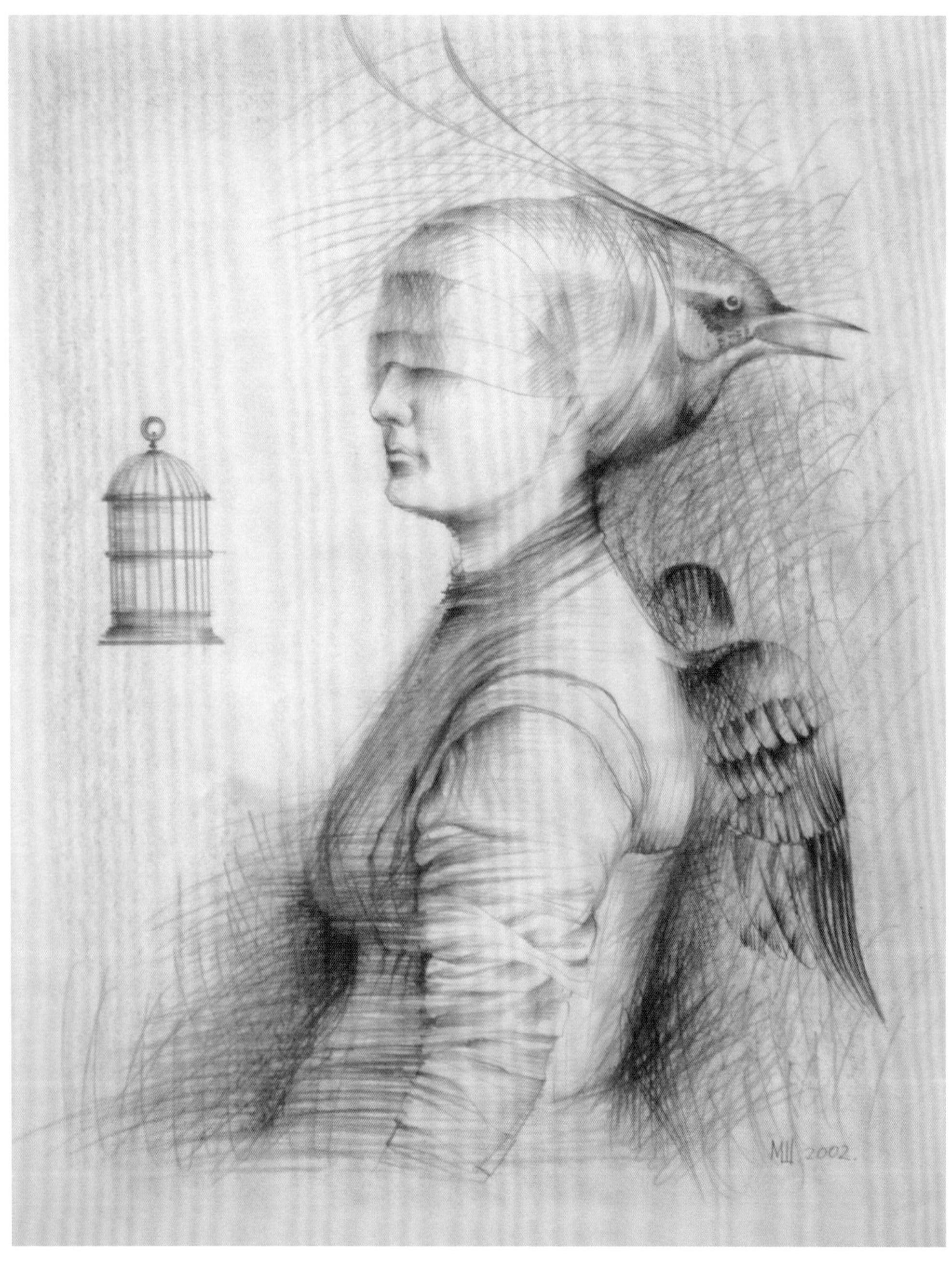

The Cage, drawing, pencil on paper, 40 × 35″ (102 × 89 cm)

Family, oil on canvas, 68 × 50″ (173 × 127 cm)

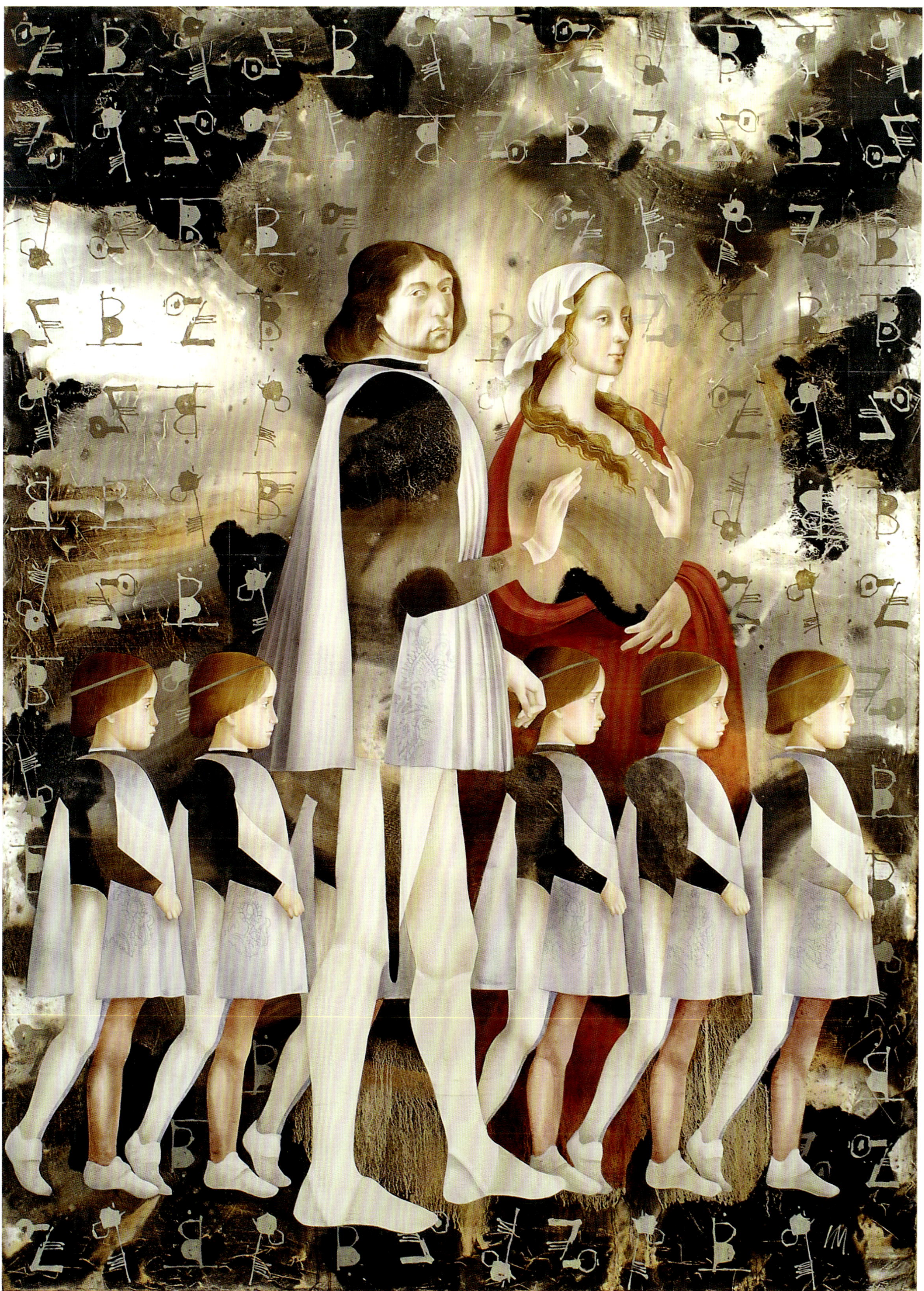

THE OTHER SIDE OF
THE LOOKING GLASS SERIES

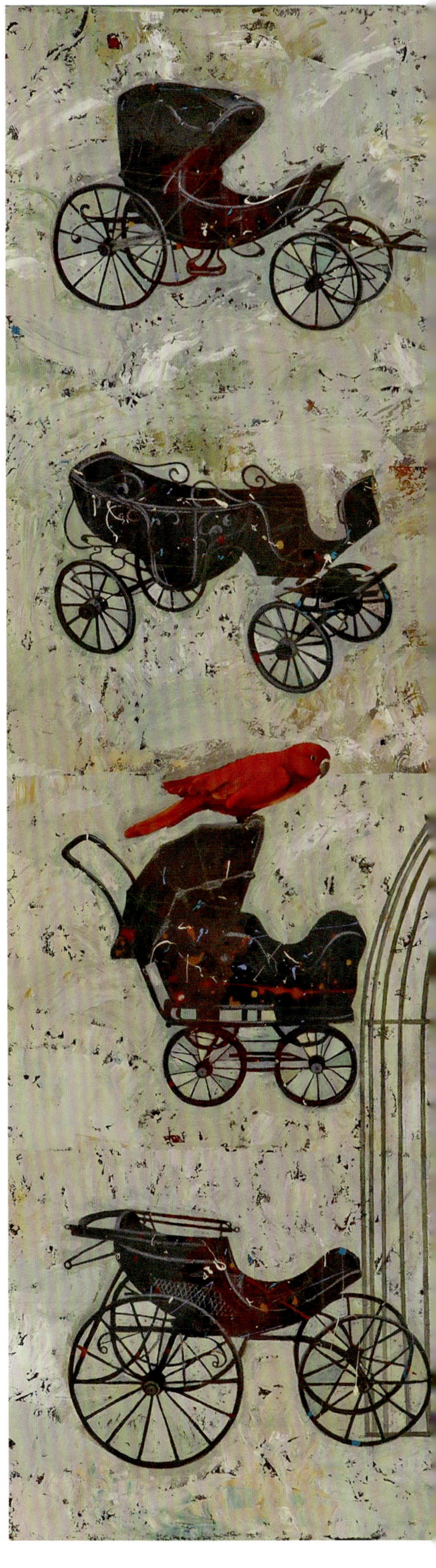

Red Queen (triptych), oil on canvas, 72 × 88″
(183 × 224 cm)

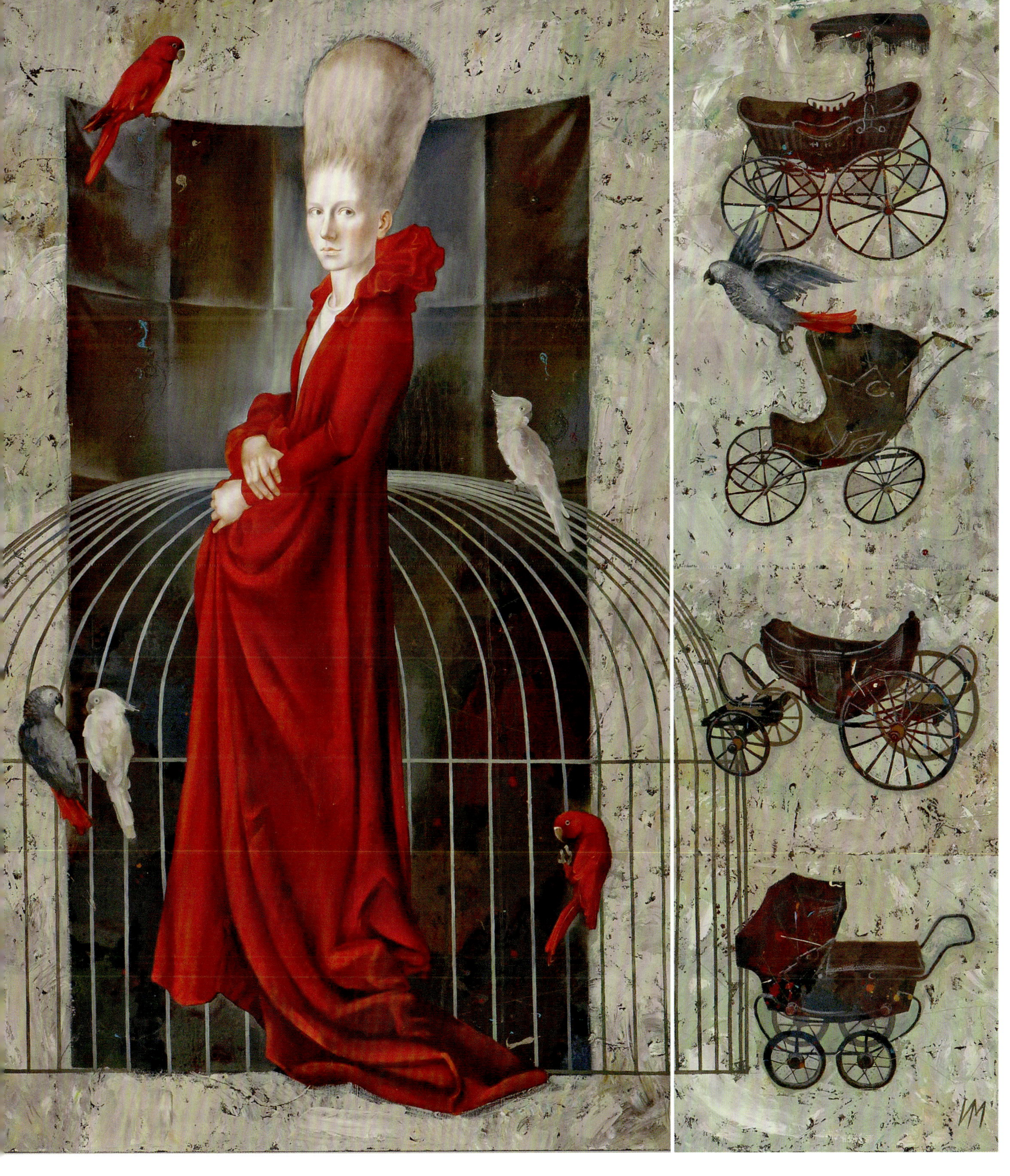

Seven Brides, oil, acrylic, 12K white gold leaf
on canvas, 64 × 86″ (163 × 218 cm)

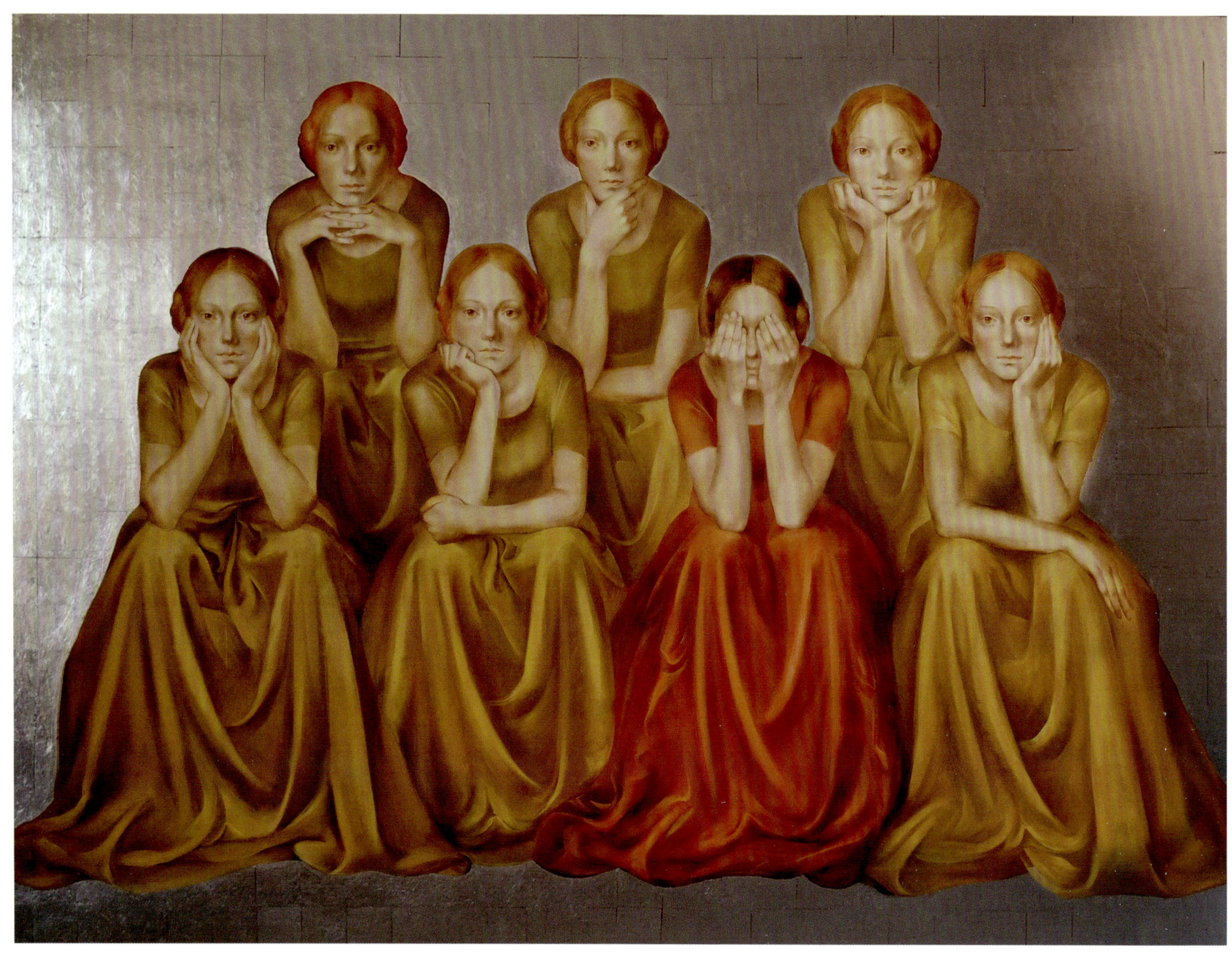

Apples for Helena, study, pencil on paper,
40 × 60" (102 × 122 cm)

Apples for Helena, oil on Belgian linen,
40 × 60" (102 × 122 cm)

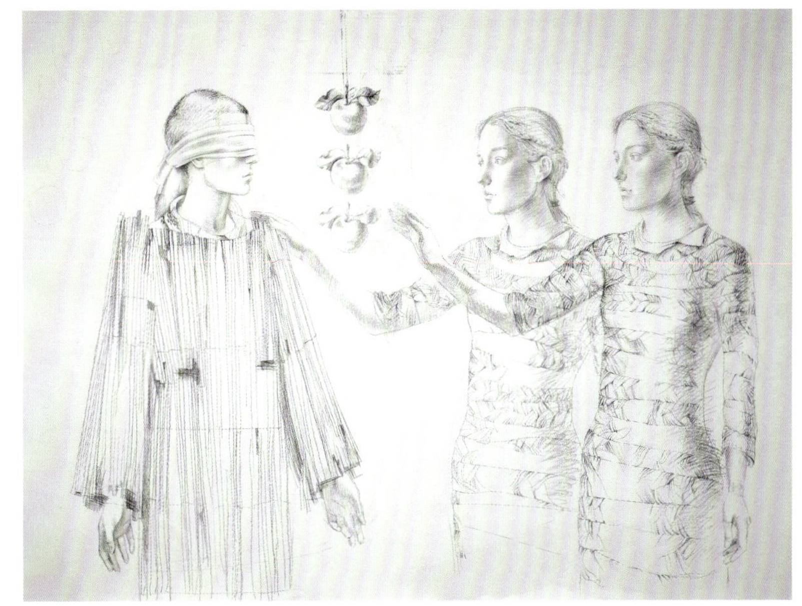

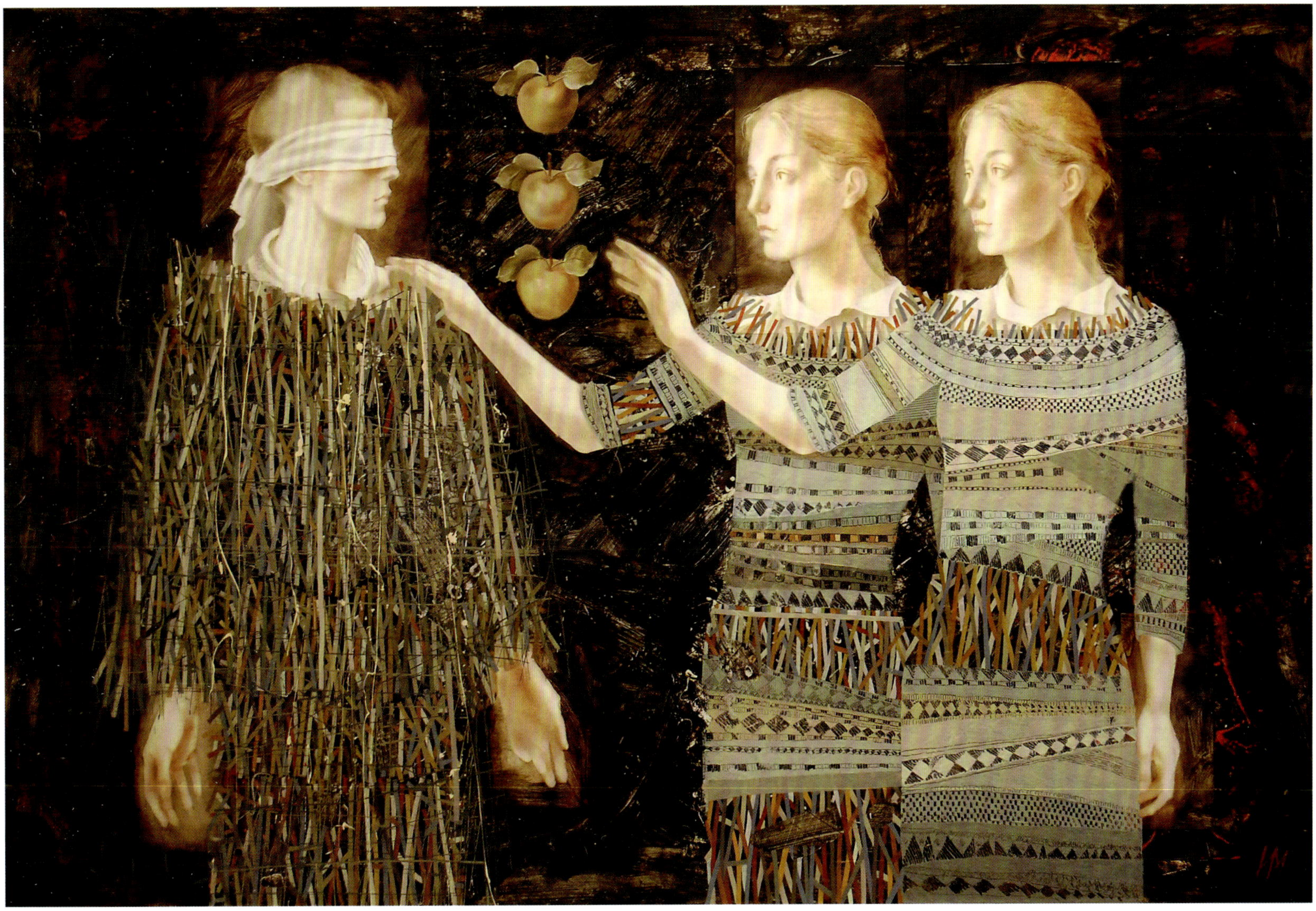

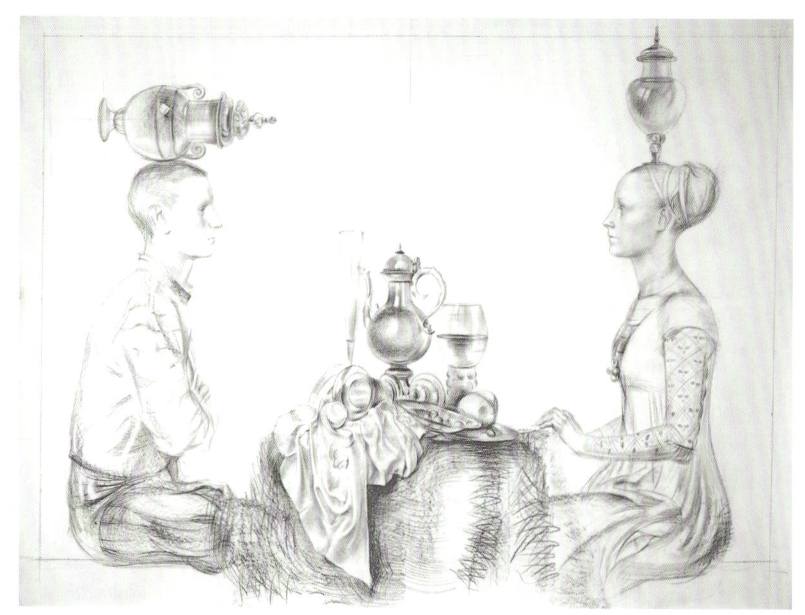

He, She & a Still-Life, drawing, pencil on paper, 48 × 64" (122 × 163 cm)

He, She & a Still-Life, oil on canvas, 48 × 64" (122 × 163 cm)

Girl & Owl (diptych), oil on canvas, 78 × 48" (198 × 122 cm)

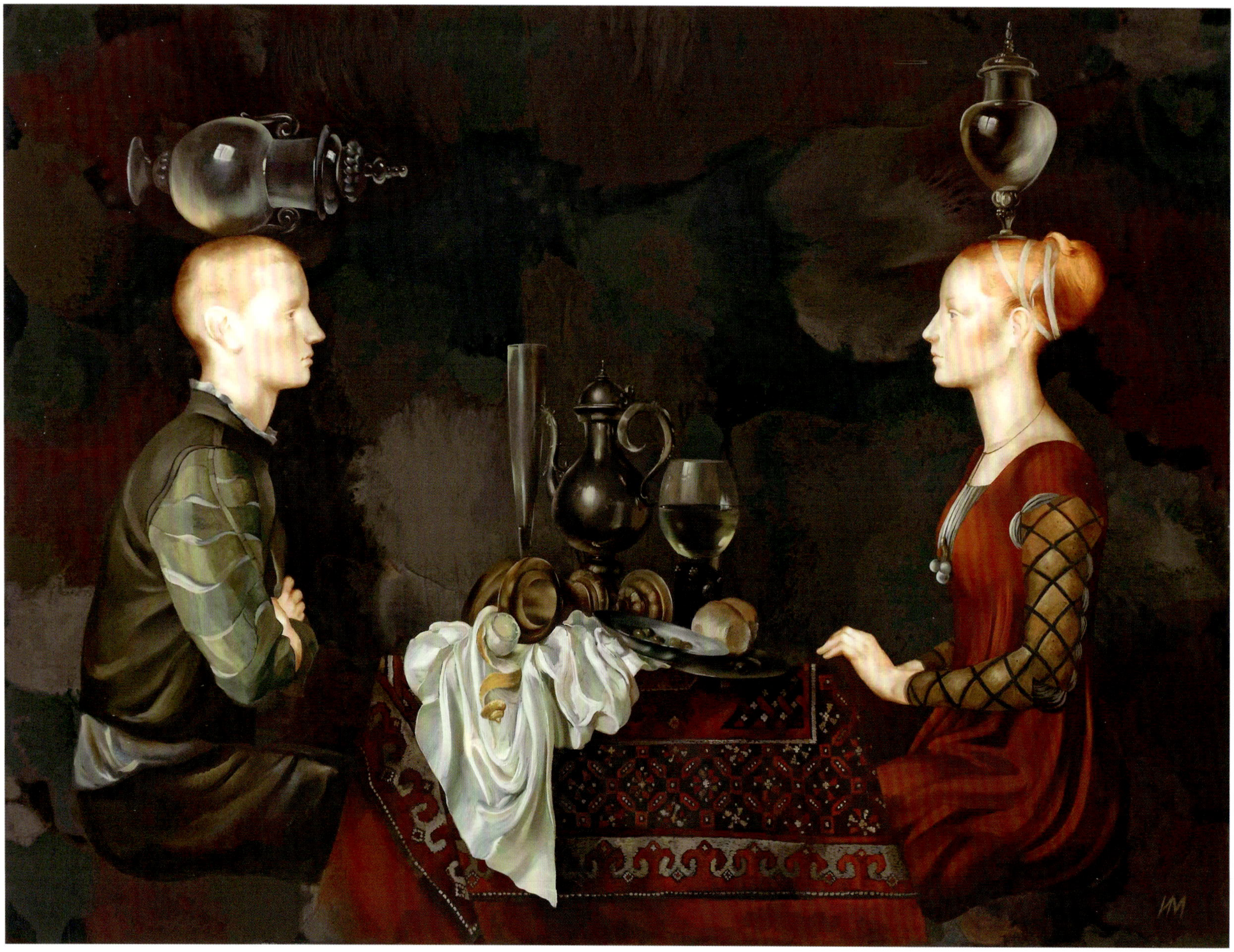

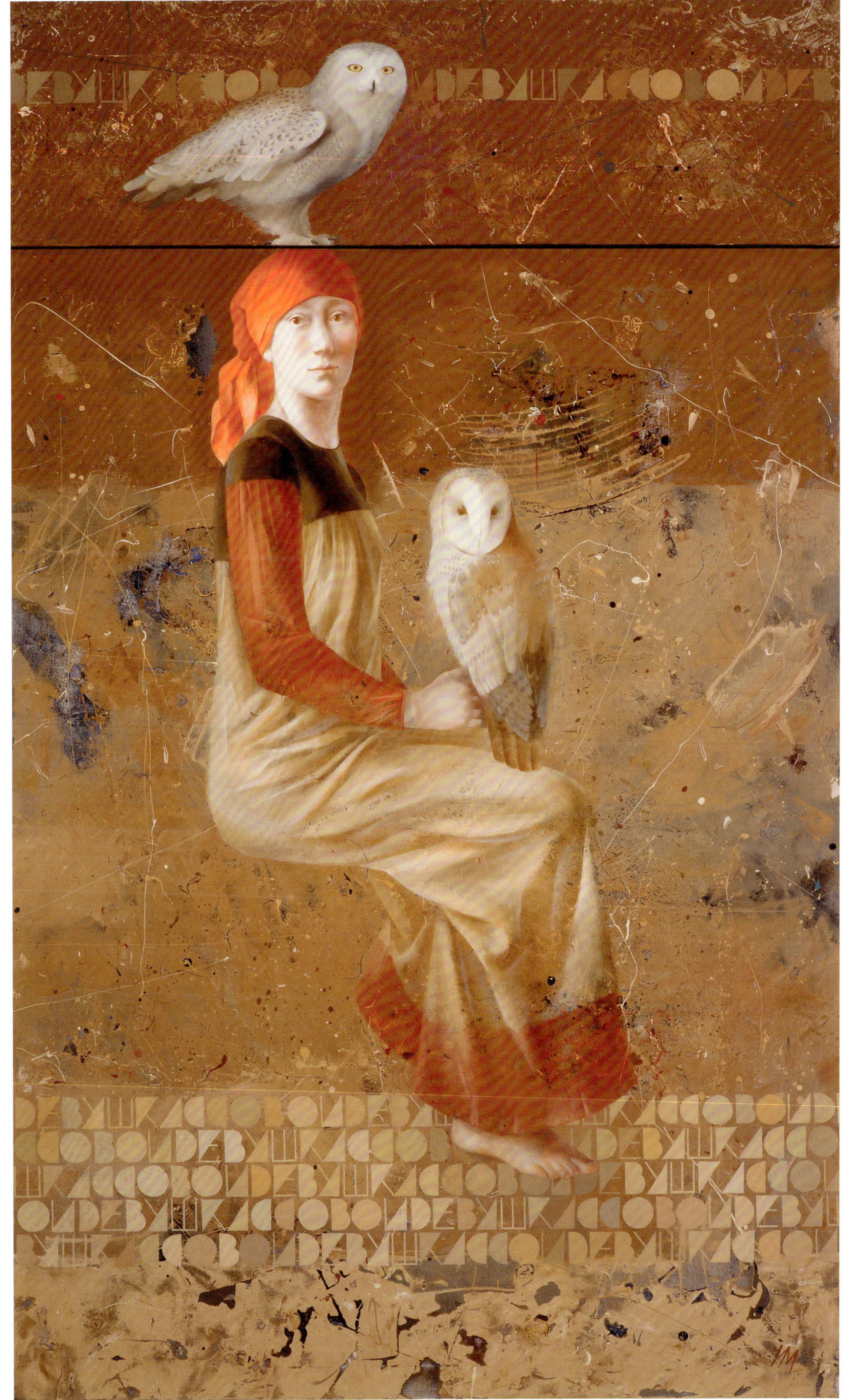

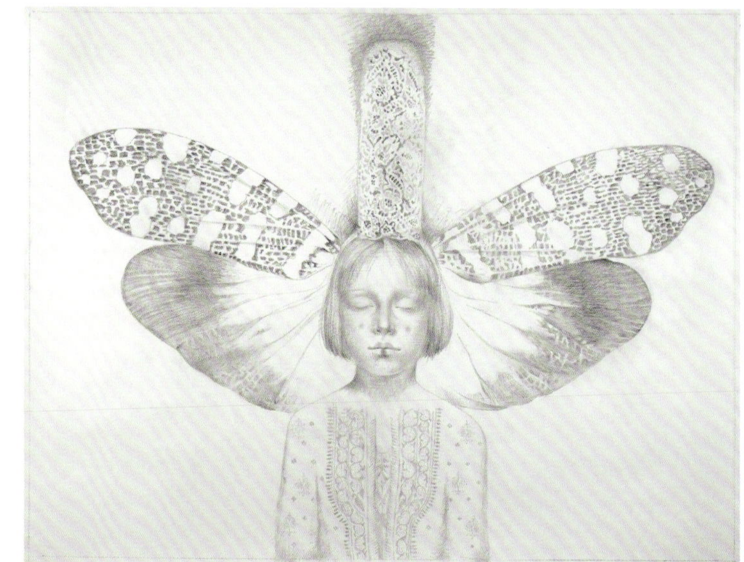

La Sylphide, study, pencil on paper, 30 × 40″
(76 × 102 cm)

La Sylphide, oil on Russian linen, 30 × 40″
(76 × 102 cm)

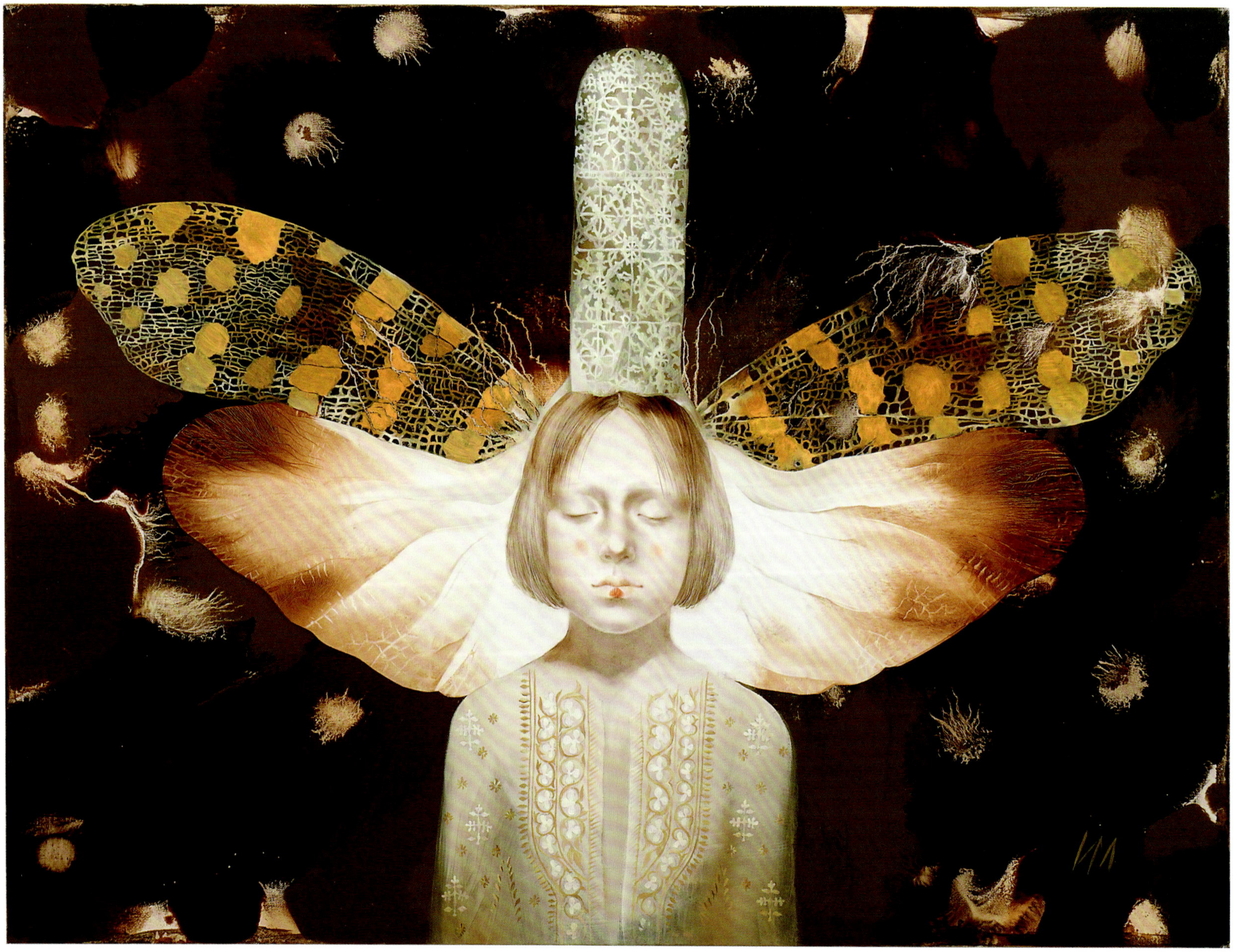

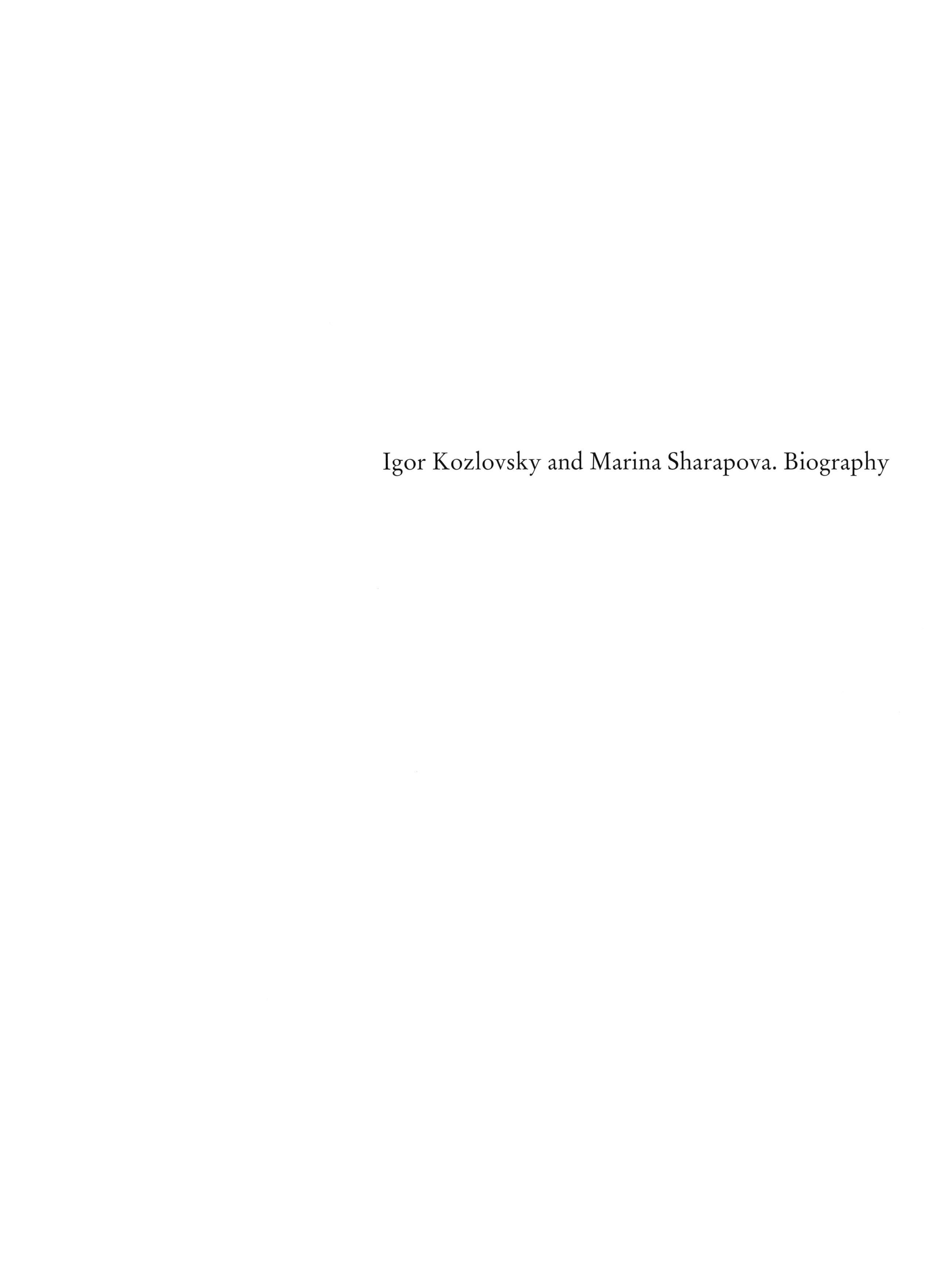

Igor Kozlovsky and Marina Sharapova. Biography

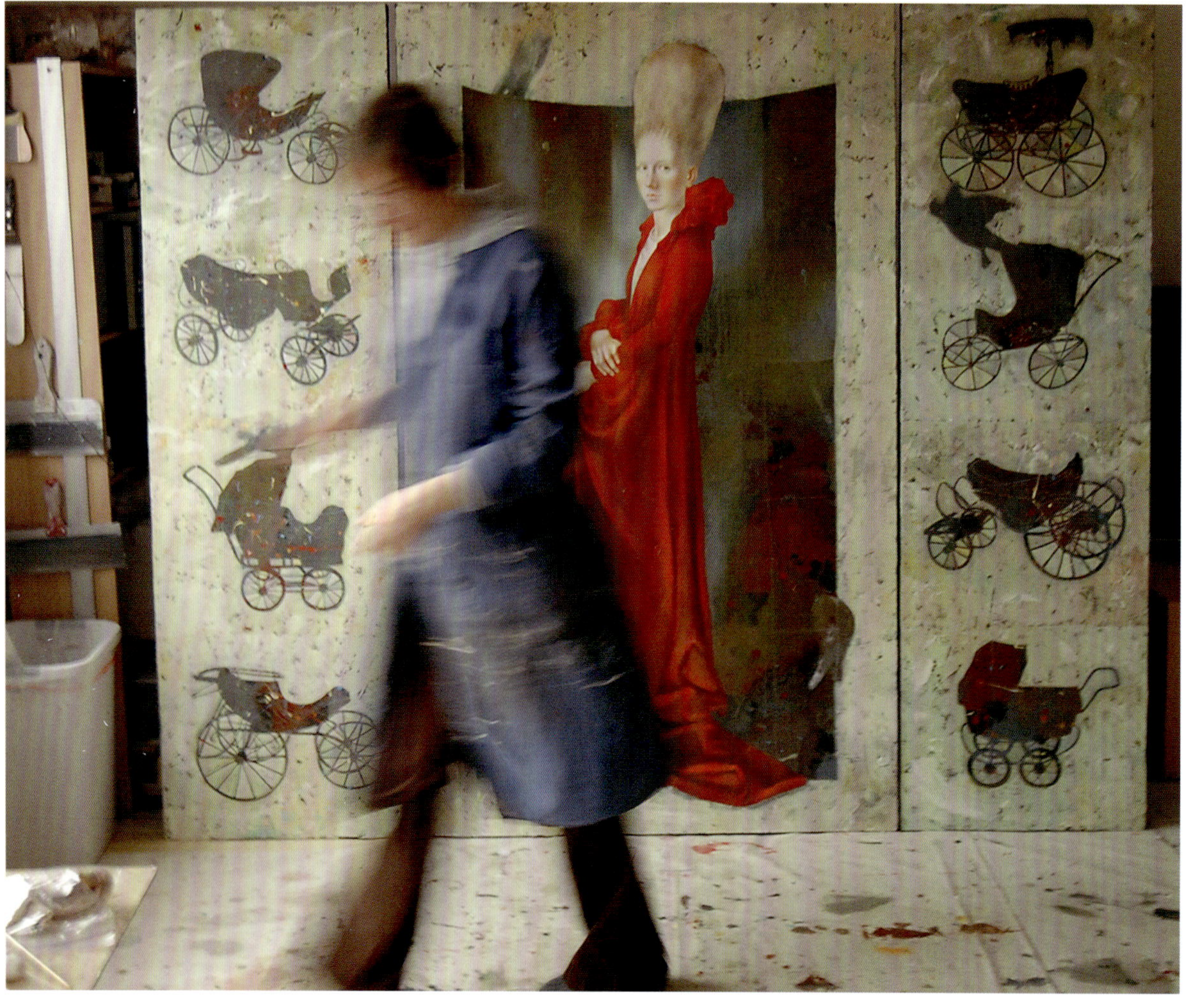

At the studio

Education

1985

MFA, Mukhina Academy of Art and Design (Baron Stieglitz's School), Saint Petersburg, Russia

Awards

2006

The Pollock-Krasner Foundation, New York, NY, USA

Two-Person Shows (partial list)

2015

Caldwell Snyder Gallery, San Francisco, CA, USA (illustrated catalog)
The Art Center, Highland Park, IL, USA (illustrated catalog)

2013

Campton Gallery, New York, NY, USA (illustrated catalog)

2012

Campton Gallery, New York, NY, USA (book published)
Chicago Cultural Center, Chicago, IL, USA

2010

Campton Gallery, New York, NY, USA (book published)

2009

Wall Street Journal, The Durst Organization (sponsor), NY, USA
Thomas Masters Gallery, Chicago, IL, USA

2008

Campton Gallery, New York, NY, USA (illustrated catalog)
Northeastern Illinois University, Chicago, IL, USA
Thomas Masters Gallery, Chicago, IL, USA

2007

Caldwell Snyder Gallery, San Francisco & St. Helena, CA, USA (illustrated catalog)
Thomas Masters Gallery, Chicago, IL, USA

2006

Campton Gallery, New York, NY, USA (illustrated catalog)
Thomas Masters Gallery, Chicago, IL, USA

2004

Thomas Masters Gallery, Chicago, IL, USA (illustrated catalog)

2002

Thomas Masters Gallery, Chicago, IL, USA

1996

Centre Culturel de St. Malo, France (illustrated catalog)
Federation of Interior Architects, St. Petersburg, Russia (illustrated catalog) (members since 1991)

1995

Consulate of France, St. Petersburg, Russia (illustrated catalog)

Group Shows (partial list)

2015–16

Janet Rady Fine Art Gallery, London, Dubai

2011

Los Angeles Art Fair (Caldwell Snyder Gallery), Los Angeles, CA, USA
SOFA Chicago (KM Fine Arts Gallery), Chicago, IL, USA
KM Fine Arts Gallery, Chicago, IL, USA

2010

Art Singapore (Caldwell Snyder Gallery), Singapore
Fine Art Asia (Caldwell Snyder Gallery), Hong Kong

2008–10

Red Dot Art Fair (Caldwell Snyder Gallery), Miami, FL, USA

2006–11

Art Chicago (Thomas Masters Gallery), Chicago, IL, USA

2005–15

Caldwell Snyder Gallery, San Francisco & St. Helena, CA, USA
Campton Gallery, New York, NY, USA

2004

NIU Art Museum, Chicago, IL, USA

2002–12

Thomas Masters Gallery, Chicago, IL, USA

1996–2012

Artemise Gallery, Dinard, France

Corporate Collections (partial list)

International Corporate Art (ICArt), Oslo, Miami, London
Regent Seven Seas Cruises, USA
S&R Foundation, Washington, DC, USA
Newmark Knight Frank, New York, NY, USA
Hendrix Allardyce, Los Angeles, CA, USA
Sara Lee Corporation, New York, NY, USA
The Durst Organization, New York, NY, USA
Hollywood's producers and actors, Los Angeles, CA, USA
Bristol Myers Squibb Company, USA
Alinea Restaurant Art Collection, Chicago, IL, USA
Potash Corporation, USA–Canada
Governor of Tokyo, Japan

Bibliography (partial list)

Igor & Marina
A first monograph, written by Ilya Kutik, translated into English by Andrew Wachtel. Editor Paola Gribaudo, published by Skira. 96 pages, 76 color plates. Milan, Italy, 2016

Vogue Italia
"Inside Igor & Marina's studio". December 2015, Italy

Pambianco
Magazine cover and a cover story. 5 images, page 103. December 2015 issue, Italy

Pambianco Beauty
Magazine cover and a cover story. 5 images, page 98. December 2015 issue, Italy

The Monthly
Magazine cover and an article. December 2015 issue, San Francisco Bay, USA

In-Magazine
"How To Work Together", magazine article by Carlos Arellano. 26 images, pages 90–135, November 2015 issue, Switzerland

Interiors the Best
"Always In Sight" , magazine article by Tatiana Fofonova. 10 images, June 2016 issue, Russia

Juxtapoz
"The Work of Igor & Marina", 16 images, October 2013 issue, USA

Igor & Marina
A coffee-table album, hardcover, 24 pages, illustrations. Published by Caldwell Snyder Gallery, first (2010) and second (2012) editions, USA

American Art Collector
"Blending Talents", two pages magazine article, four images. April 2012 issue, USA

The Artist's Magazine
"Beautiful Ambiguity", magazine cover plus eight pages magazine article by Ruth K. Meyer, 17 images. 2009, USA

Luxe
"Artistic Tango", two pages coffee-table magazine article by Brielle M. Ferreira, including full page of artists' portraits, taken by celebrity photographer Mark Hauser. 2009, USA

New World of Art
"A Couple In One Boat", two pages magazine article by Alexander Kotlomanov, 3 images. 2008, Saint Petersburg, Russia

Gallery Guide
Full page back cover plus full-page article: Spotlight: "Igor & Marina 'Under The Renaissance Sky'", by Caldwell Snyder Gallery, 2007, San Francisco, CA, USA

Evanston Review
Pioneer Press: "A Couple With Artistic Chemistry", full-page article of Chicago North Shore's paper, 2 images, by Robert Loerzel, 2005, USA

Design & Architecture
Chicago Edition magazine, 1 image in an article "Ms. Congeniality", by Lisa Skolnik 2004. Chicago, IL, USA

Shelter Chicago
"Marina Sharapova & Igor Kozlovsky: Visions of A Renaissance That Never Was", magazine article by Carol Tisch, pages 50–57, 10 images, 2003, Chicago, IL, USA

Evanston Review
Pioneer Press: "Couple Marries Artistic Styles", full-page article of Chicago North Shore's paper, 3 images, by Ellen Pritsker, 2002, USA

Chicago Home & Garden
"Amber Waves", magazine article by Kelly Aiglon, 2002, Chicago, IL, USA

Nathalie
French-Russian Magazine article by Margarita Kostrits, IAAC, Curator of Contemporary Art, State Russian Museum, 1996, St. Petersburg, Russia